House Cleaning

How to Get Your Kids Begging for Chores

(The Ultimate Guide to Get Your Home Always Perfectly Clean)

Dwain Carberry

Published By **Chris David**

Dwain Carberry

House Cleaning: How to Get Your Kids Begging for Chores (The Ultimate Guide to Get Your Home Always Perfectly Clean)

ISBN   978-1-998038-15-2

No part of this guidebook shall be reproduced in any form without permission in writing from the publisher except in the case of brief quotations embodied in critical articles or reviews.

Legal & Disclaimer

The information contained in this book is not designed to replace or take the place of any form of medicine or professional medical advice. The information in this book has been provided for educational & entertainment purposes only.

The information contained in this book has been compiled from sources deemed reliable, and it is accurate to the best of the Author's knowledge; however, the Author cannot guarantee its accuracy and validity and cannot be held liable for any errors or omissions. Changes are periodically made to this book. You must consult your doctor or get professional medical advice before using any of the suggested remedies, techniques, or information in this book.

Upon using the information contained in this book, you agree to hold harmless the Author from and against any damages, costs, and expenses, including any legal fees potentially resulting from the application of any of the information provided by this guide. This disclaimer applies to any damages or injury caused by the use and application, whether directly or indirectly, of any advice or information presented, whether for breach of contract, tort, negligence, personal injury, criminal intent, or under any other cause of action.

You agree to accept all risks of using the information presented inside this book. You need to consult a professional medical practitioner in order to ensure you are both able and healthy enough to participate in this program.

Table Of Contents

Chapter 1: Tips BEFORE Cleaning and Organizing your Home

To make cleansing and organizing your home more systematic, you need to plot the assignment in advance. This will keep you from feeling beaten with all of the matters that you want to do. By planning the duties well, you may be capable of maximize it sluggish as a manner to provide you with hundreds of time to do exceptional subjects. After all, cleaning and organizing your own home isn't always the best undertaking that you want to do. It is truely one of the many chores that wives need to do each day. Below is a list of tips which you want to do earlier than cleaning and organizing your private home.

Schedule your easy up

If you're a busy mom, that you maximum possibly are, you need to time table the clean up so you can awareness all your attention on cleansing and corporation. If you just do it whenever you want or every time you have had been given quick loose time and you could squeeze cleansing and organizing for an hour or so, you could not have the capability to complete and you could experience more burdened out because of the reality you have got got first rate activities. It is crucial to set a schedule this is most handy for you.

For strolling better halves, the brilliant time to schedule your sizable cleansing and industrial employer agency is on weekends or on your relaxation days whilst you're at domestic. This way, you aren't worn-out from artwork and your mind is likewise targeted at the challenge at hand. If you do not need the youngsters to be there at the same time as you're cleaning, you can report for a holiday leave on a weekday for this reason.

For housewives, it's miles pleasant to schedule the clean up even as the children are at university and anyone else is out so that you have the whole residence to your self and those aren't inside the way. It is probably tough to clean if you furthermore have to attend to your little one or if you typically need to prevent due to the fact a person has to apply the toilet.

You do no longer always need to do the whole thing in within the future in particular if your property is big. You can time table the easy up for numerous days so that you will not revel in too worn-out.

Ask for help

You do no longer have to do the entirety yourself even though you are attempting to turn out to be the quality partner. Remember, you can nonetheless ask for assist from other members of your family even in case you are vying for the correct spouse identify. After all, you're all residing within the identical residence and it's far their home as loads as yours. Older children can already assist out with the useful resource of selecting up their clutter or dusting off surfaces the usage of a easy cloth or feather duster. Teenagers can assist with extra hard obligations together with vacuuming, cleaning small home machine, and organizing.

You also can ask your older children to attend to their more youthful siblings at the equal time as you are cleaning the house. Your husband assist you to carry heavy furniture and domestic device and may do the upkeep and fixes in your house. If you have were given teens, you do not actually need to easy their personal bedrooms because of the fact they might do it by way of themselves. This will not high-quality make your interest less difficult but it's going to additionally educate them to be accountable.

Do it one room or area at a time

To make the undertaking before you a lot much less overwhelming, you must do not forget cleansing the house one room at a time. You need to moreover consider starting from the indoors in advance than going out. If you have got were given a 2nd ground, you need to begin from the second one floor before you smooth the rooms downstairs.

For example, you may start cleaning the bathrooms, bedrooms, kitchen, eating room, living room, and hallways earlier than you circulate on in your outside regions like your patio, garage, and outside. Depending on the size, you could spend some hours as a good deal as an entire day to smooth one room or location. This will make cleaning and organizing your property extra systematic.

Make a checklist

You have to recollect making geared up a checklist especially when you have such a whole lot of sports so you will not forget some thing. When making a checklist, you may write down the tasks which you want to finish room via room. For instance, even as cleaning the bed room, you could listing down tasks along with dust the ceiling, update curtains and bed linens, make the bed, arrange the closet, dirt surfaces, and vacuum the floor. This will can help you recognize what nevertheless wishes to be completed a terrific way to save you you from dawdling in one task longer than essential.

Whenever you go out one venture to your list, it will offer you with a experience of fulfillment due to the truth you apprehend which you have already finished something and your responsibilities have become fewer and lots less. If you delegate some of the responsibilities for your husband and kids, you need to moreover recollect giving them a checklist truly so they may no longer neglect what they need to do.

Prepare all your cleaning resources

Before you even begin cleaning, make sure which you've have been given the critical cleaning additives to make your property spotless. You probably already have the easy cleansing resources along with vacuum, mop, small rags, feather duster, squeegee, chemical cleaners, disinfectants, and air fresheners. You can also additionally need a ladder, bucket, restore equipment, and paint.

For the outdoor, you need gardening system which includes broom, garden scissors, garden mower, shovel, sprinkler, and rake. It is vital to check if you have all the subjects that you want for cleansing to keep away from dropping your precious time seeking out a device or deliver that you want at the same time as you are already in the method of cleansing your own home.

Get the right storage gadgets

When it involves retaining your private home prepared, you want to have the proper storage gadgets to offer your things their respective houses. You need cabinets in your books; a document case to your documents and folders; drawers for your underwear and socks; particular racks to your footwear, spices, and wine; boxes and containers to your kids's toys; laundry basket or prevent on your dirty garments; and different storage gadgets that you assume you want to keep all of the rooms of your house litter-free.

More frequently than now not, the residence appears messy and unkempt not due to the reality it's far dirty however due to the litter that litters the desk, mattress, counter, or floor. By without a doubt de-cluttering your private home, your own home will proper away appearance better and nicer.

Renovate and repair

This is non-compulsory but in case you are planning to renovate your home whenever speedy, you need to do it first before cleaning. This way, you do not need to easy and installation your property once more after the protection. Renovations include changing your floors, making the room larger, together with a wall department, repainting the walls, putting in integrated domestic device and fixtures, and so forth.

If there are topics that need to be repaired in your own home, collectively with the broken dishwasher, damaged heater, or the unsightly hole at the wall or floors, you need to get the ones out of the manner first so you can recognition all your hobby on cleaning and organizing. It is hard to clean and put together if you are though looking for some aspect to finish. You may have your husband do the maintenance for you or you could hire a professional repairperson mainly for added complicated fixes associated with plumbing and electric wiring.

These are the matters which you need to do while planning for current home cleansing and organisation. By doing the recommendations above in advance than cleaning and organizing your home, your obligations will become a lot less hard due to the truth everything is nicely-deliberate and you are getting help out of your circle of relatives contributors. The next bankruptcy will provide you with a few realistic hints on the equal time as you're inside the manner of cleaning and organizing your property.

Chapter 2: Tips DURING Cleaning and Organizing Your Home

In this chapter, you'll look at some useful hints and mind that you could attempt during the whole manner of cleaning and organizing your home. These tips will make this apparently daunting chore easier and greater fun. Imagine cleansing the house and having fun at the equal time. This will encourage you to smooth the residence greater often and could train the child that cleansing the residence isn't so tough and tedious anyhow. You can attempt the subsequent tips in the list beneath.

Play a few tune

Any house chore turns into extra a laugh if you are doing it on the same time as being attentive to track. You can turn on the radio to your favourite station or play your favorite albums of all time. If you do now not want to disturb different human beings in the house, like even as your infant is sound asleep and also you do not need to wake him up, you can additionally play songs in your MP3 participant which you could supply with you anywhere you move. You can play upbeat tune to keep you energized while cleaning.

There will definitely be a soar in the doorstep even at the identical time as you are cleansing if you are being attentive to upbeat song or to your chosen songs. Your mind may even not be within the task handy but inside the tune that you are taking note of especially if you apprehend the lyrics through manner of coronary heart and also you can't assist yourself however sing whilst cleaning. This will make the time fly speedy and in advance than you know it, you have got were given wiped smooth the entire residence with out feeling exhausted.

Play video video games

To make cleansing and organizing your private home more fun and thrilling not simplest for you but moreover to your kids, you should recall playing video video games on the same time as cleaning. You can turn this chore right into a beat-the-clock form of hobby in that you have to finish cleaning and organizing each room in an hour or so. You need to furthermore do the same component together with your kids who are cleaning their personal bedrooms. Tell them that it's miles a competition and whoever has the cleanest room within the shortest time will win a prize. You can choose a prize for your self which encompass giving yourself a snack smash or you can supply fun prizes in your youngsters.

Take a destroy

You want to additionally take brief breaks from time to time to offer your self a hazard to recharge even for just a quick time. After cleansing for an hour immediately, you can take a quick 15-minute break to just sit down and lighten up on a chair on the same time as consuming a snack. You also can take a wreck each time you sense worn-out otherwise you experience like you're already losing steam. Your breaks do no longer continually ought to be scheduled. You should put together your snacks earlier and make sure that they come up with energy to hold you going. You can put together crackers and cheese, energy bars, path blend, a pitcher of freshly squeezed juice, or a cup of heat tea.

Do not get aspect tracked

Many matters can get you side tracked even as you're cleansing and organizing your private home which encompass searching TV or checking your e mail, Facebook, or Twitter. This is why it's far critical to expose off the TV and your laptop to keep yourself from getting distracted from what you're doing. If the TV is grew to become on and a cable channel starts offevolved offevolved showing a outstanding movie that you were planning to examine, you could discover yourself sitting in front of the TV set and forgetting which you but want to smooth and set up your private home.

This is also real at the same time as you go browsing. When you log in to your Facebook net net web page, a chum might ship you a speak message and also you can't assist but supply a respond till you do not apprehend which you have already spent an hour or so chatting in place of cleansing up.

Bring all of the cleansing additives which you want

Instead of going to and fro to and from the cleaning supply cupboard, you need to don't forget bringing all of the factors that you want in a basket or a caddy to hold time and electricity. For instance, in case you are cleaning your bed room, ensure to supply the vacuum, feather duster, trash bag, and air freshener with you earlier than you start.

Choose a place to start

As what has been noted in advance, you could begin from the inner of the residence to the outside regions or you can begin from the second one ground to the ground floor. You also can start from top to bottom or from the ceiling to the floor. You need to moreover do dry cleaning first along with dusting and organizing in advance than you do the moist cleansing to preserve dirt and lint from sticking on wet surfaces.

Some people also choose to begin with their least favored room or the maximum tough to easy in advance than they skip without delay to the most favored or simplest to clean. You can also begin from the maximum crucial place to easy in advance than transferring at once to the no longer so essential rooms and areas in your home.

Bring a trash bag and a basket with you

You will want a trash bag everywhere you bypass because that is in that you're going to placed the trash that wants to be thrown out. You must also bring a basket wherein you could located topics that need to be moved to their proper places. For example, while cleaning the bedroom, you may located the grimy garments within the basket so that you can supply it in some time to the laundry vicinity.

You also can deliver grimy coffee cups and saucers from the residing room to the kitchen abruptly when you have a basket with you. This will make it easier that allows you to deliver a couple of matters and bring them to their respective rooms.

Be careful

When cleansing the residence, you want to be cautious because injuries can take region which can reason harm and damage to your fixtures and domestic device. For example, at the same time as handling chemical cleaners, you need to put on a mask and a couple of rubber gloves to protect yourself from the poisonous fumes and to hold your pores and skin blanketed from the substance. If you will use a ladder to easy the ceiling, you need to make sure that the ladder is robust. Better but, ask someone to keep the ladder for you whilst you are hiking on it.

You must furthermore make sure that your arms are dry in advance than plugging the vacuum or any electrical home device to save you electrocution. If you're using the vacuum, you should close to the door to maintain your children and pets from entering into the room and via accident tripping at the wire on the equal time as you are vacuuming. This can also preserve them from getting uncovered to chemical cleaners, dirt, and dirt that can be harmful to their health.

Chapter 3: Tips AFTER Cleaning and Organizing Your Home

There are although hundreds of factors which you want to do when you are finished cleaning and organizing your private home. These subjects will assist you emerge as brought on to hold with what you've got got were given started and function a regular time table for cleaning and organizing your home. They may also help you hold your smooth and prepared home. Below is a list of things which you need to do after you are finished cleaning and organizing your private home.

Reward yourself

After an extended day of cleansing and organizing your property, you want to supply yourself a pat on the yet again and a reward of your choice. You can reward yourself with the useful aid of soaking in a warm aromatic bubble tub or through using going out for dinner in preference to cooking. You can also reward your self through inviting your buddies over a good way to reward you in your appropriate house duties. Choose a reward as a manner to maintain you caused to do normal cutting-edge cleansing and agency.

You can continually tie your easy up with a praise so that you should have some trouble to sit up for even as cleaning. You ought to hold in thoughts to praise yourself for a activity well completed and for keeping your own home smooth and tidy for yourself and your family. Moreover, a smooth and tidy home is already a praise in itself as it allows you to lighten up and unwind and spend a stress-free night time collectively along with your own family as soon as anybody is lower decrease again from paintings or university.

Put away your cleaning materials

Once you are finished cleansing the house, you want to put away all of the cleaning resources and keep them within the cleaning deliver closet. You do not need your vacuum or broom lying throughout the residence once you are completed because it beats the motive of getting a modern domestic cleaning and employer business enterprise. You need to additionally save cleansing gear and materials right away due to the truth you do no longer want your toddler or puppy to play with these items.

These may be dangerous to their health not handiest due to the fact they may be dirty but furthermore because those chemical cleaners are poisonous. Make wonderful which you have a storage closet or cabinet for all your cleaning property in which you may with out issue locate and get them the next time you decide to clean and set up your house once more.

Maintain the cleanliness and tidiness

You can do quite numerous of things to be able to can help you hold the cleanliness and tidiness after doing the general cleansing and business enterprise together with the ones indexed below.

• You should discover ways to clean as you bypass so you do not want to smooth hundreds whilst you time table a trendy smooth up. Pick up the litter that you may discover each day and positioned them lower returned of their respective places. You ought to additionally smooth the floor everyday via mopping or sweeping the dust and dust. This way, dust and dirt do not accumulate over time which makes it less hard for you at the same time as you make a decision to easy up very well.

• Another tip is to do small cleansing regularly. You do now not need to smooth each nook and cranny of your property each day or every weekend. Just ensure that you time table everyday 'clean sweep' normal certainly to maintain your property neat and tidy. You do not want to examine for your once-a-month popular clean up in that you clean the house from top to backside and inner out earlier than you choose up the mop or vacuum to tidy up the place a hint bit.

• Always de-litter your fridge. You should try this often no longer nice that will help you locate what you are searching out extra resultseasily however moreover to make sure that the food inside the refrigerator are despite the fact that eatable.

• If you have got have been given a everyday technique, make it a factor to do a 'easy sweep' earlier than going to mattress. You want to moreover avoid leaving dirty dishes within the sink in advance than drowsing so you do not have a few thing to worry about even as you awaken within the morning.

• Upon waking up inside the morning, you should make your mattress proper away because of the truth an unmade bed makes a bed room appearance cluttered.

• Enroll in automatic payments and unsubscribe from vain magazines to lessen junk mails that only upload up for your muddle.

• Do not buy matters that you in reality do not need to avoid cluttering your house. You want to furthermore often purge matters which you no longer want or need to de-litter your own home which encompass antique garments, antique magazines, vintage books, and so forth.

Create clean up guidelines for the entire own family

Now that the house is all all over again tidy and spotless, you need to consider making rules so as to assist preserve the cleanliness. For instance, you need to deliver a basket to each of your youngsters in which they are able to located their matters which might be cluttering the dwelling room to be placed decrease back in their respective bedrooms. You should additionally make a rule approximately setting lower back everything in their proper locations in order that de-cluttering and cleaning can be a lot a whole lot less complicated.

You need to additionally assign responsibilities to each member of the family. They can wash the dirty dishes, take out the trash, set up the table for dinner, and so on. There are such a lot of policies that you could offer you with that assist you to keep a easy and tidy home.

Invest in immoderate exceptional cleaning machine

If you need to make cleansing and employer less difficult and extra inexperienced, you need to undergo in mind making an investment in excessive tremendous tool that could do the challenge for you. For instance, if you have a big lawn, you need to remember making an investment in a experience-on garden mower to make it less complex on the manner to reduce the grass in your property. You need to additionally put money into a high powered vacuum this is green in cleansing your large house.

These cleansing machine can be high-priced but the rate tag is certainly nicely worth it at the same time as you notice how loads much less tough your duties is probably. They moreover very last for an extended time than those cheap cleaning machines which means that that you do not really want to spend cash to replace them for many years to come back. You must do your research on-line and observe critiques to know which cleansing device is the extremely good preference for your cleaning desires.

You want to recall doing the ones guidelines after you are performed with the general smooth up and commercial enterprise company to prepare your self for the subsequent smooth up. These suggestions will make your hobby masses easier the following time you time desk every different thorough clean up. The following couple of chapters will provide you with greater useful tips on a way to smooth and put together every room or place of your house.

Chapter 4: Cleaning and Organizing your Bedroom

Your mattress room is your non-public vicinity so ensure that it's far usually easy and organized. You can smooth the master's mattress room in that you and your husband sleep and furthermore your younger kids' bedrooms and tourist rooms. If you have older kids and that they have their non-public bed room, you ought to tell them that they may be accountable for cleaning their personal room. After all, they do no longer want you searching through their stuff, do they? Here are a few fashionable hints for cleansing the draw close's bedrooms and top notch bedrooms in your own home.

Make the bed

The bed is usually the focal point of a bed room. It occupies a large place in your mattress room and also you need to ensure that it is constantly made. Turn over the bed and cowl it with new mattress sheets and mattress linens. Change the pillow covers and installation them well. By in reality making the mattress, your room will proper away appearance easy and tidy.

Dust the surfaces

You can use a microfiber fabric to remove dust from the ceiling, lighting, and extraordinary surfaces that want dusting. Microfiber material is a high-quality cloth due to the reality dust debris stay with it like as if it's miles product of metal and the fabric is a magnet. You must moreover push the bed to 1 aspect so you can vacuum the floor underneath. You have probable gathered masses of dust bunnies beneath your mattress particularly if you have not moved your mattress for years. You need to vacuum the whole floor to take away dust and dirt particles.

Change curtains

You need to additionally keep in mind changing your curtains to straight away supply your bed room a today's appearance. If you're using blinds, you need to take it down and wash it with water and cleansing soap to remove dirt and dirt. You can replace the curtains on your mattress room at least as quickly as a month. For included curtains which can be made from non-washing device-pleasant materials, you may honestly vacuum or dry smooth them in vicinity of washing them with cleaning cleaning soap and water because of the fact the ones can damage them.

Organize your closet

One of the largest demanding conditions close to cleansing and organizing your bed room is organizing your closet. This is specially right if you have hundreds of garments and footwear. However, you want to tackle this mission to make it much less complicated on the way to find out what you are searching out. Here are the topics which you want to do even as organizing your closet.

• Take out all your garments and fold them properly. Group comparable clothes collectively including t-shirts, shorts, pants, and underclothes. Some even bypass as an extended way as coloration coding their clothes. You exceptional want to fold those that you are not going to grasp.

• Hang blouses, jeans, skirts, match, get dressed shirts, jackets, and dresses nicely. Make effective which you hold them properly to save you them from turning into deformed. When setting jeans, you may label them one after the other to make it less complex that allows you to discover what you are looking for.

Just write the fashion at the tag like boot reduce, skinny, immediately cut, and so forth and the emblem and distinctive statistics that you assume is essential.

• For small apparel objects like underwear, socks, handkerchiefs, and ties, fold them nicely in a drawer. You can also put them in a separate fabric cloth wardrobe in case your closet does no longer have a drawer.

• If you've got a massive closet, you may additionally prepare your shoes internal. They want to have a separate shelf or rack. You can take them out of the field and display them or you could go away them in the field earlier than placing them to your closet. Storing them in the box is a extraordinary location saving technique however it could be tough for you at the same time as you want to find out the right pair of footwear for your outfit. What you can do is to take a image of the shoes and stick the image on the field to will let you understand what's internal. This way, you do now not want to open them one by one simply to discover what you're seeking out. If your closet is small, you can set up them in a separate shelf or rack for your bed room.

• You must furthermore put together your accessories. You can located the high priced ones in a jewelry area or case or you can create an accessory organizer wherein you may draw near your necklaces, bracelets, and prolonged earrings.

• Always de-litter your closet through the use of having rid of factors which you now not placed on due to the truth they may be now not your fashion or due to the fact they do no longer fit your needs anymore. If you haven't worn a few thing for over a year, you need to get rid of it due to the fact you are not going to position on it each time short. You have to additionally have containers or packing containers for seasonal clothes like iciness garments, swimsuits, and sports sports activities garments.

De-litter your mattress room

Aside from your closet, you need to moreover installation various things on your mattress room together with your books and other shows. You need to have a bedside desk with a drawer wherein you could placed the lamp, your cell smartphone, analyzing glasses, and the book which you are reading.

Chapter 5: Cleaning and Organizing your Bathroom

Another vital part of your home is the toilet due to the reality that is in which you could unwind with the resource of the usage of taking a bath and that is additionally in which you smooth and relive yourself. How ironic it might be if the vicinity wherein you're alleged to wash yourself is grimy. You should make certain that your bathroom is clean mainly if you and your associate percentage the equal rest room. Here are a few elegant hints for cleaning the relaxation room.

Get rid of factors that do not belong inside the relaxation room

Remove the grimy clothes, footwear, books, and exceptional subjects that don't belong inside the relaxation room in advance than you start cleaning. Cleaning the rest room calls for water so make certain to take out anything which you do no longer need to get wet. You can throw trash which consist of empty soap boxes and shampoo bottles inside the trash bin in advance than you begin cleansing.

De-muddle your relaxation room

You want to have unique storage in your makeup, splendor products, toiletries, hairdryer, hair iron, curlers, and different knick knacks which you commonly have in the lavatory. You need to maintain them in a drawer wherein they may be out of sight. Throw away expired makeups and empty bottles to maintain your drawers organized. You need to furthermore keep easy towels in a shelf so that you do no longer need to exit of the toilet even as you need a modern towel.

Install storage gadgets close to your tub, rest room, bathe vicinity, and sink for the topics that you generally use at the same time as in those unique regions which incorporates bubble bath and tub oil at the identical time as taking a bath, cleaning soap and shampoo whilst taking a shower, hand cleansing cleaning soap inside the rest room, and toothbrushes and toothpaste in the sink. You need to additionally have garage for your bathroom cleansing sources under the sink.

Dust surfaces

Wipe off dirt from furniture collectively with cabinets, lighting fixtures, and countertop. You have to also wipe the mirror with a damp, lint-loose fabric. Wipe the the the the front and pinnacle of your toilet shelves and drawers. Leave the dirt and one-of-a-kind dirt debris on the floor earlier than in the long run sweeping them up later.

Clean with scrub powder

Scrub powder works for areas which might be specially grimy. You can use this to do away with dust and dust buildup within the sink and bath or spherical faucets. Sprinkle those areas with scrub powder and depart for about 15 minutes. You can do diverse matters at the identical time as looking for the 15 minutes to end which embody removing the trash or dusting off surfaces. After 15 minutes, scrub off the grimy regions the use of a broom with difficult bristles.

Clean the toilet

Cleaning the rest room is one of the most tough obligations with regards to cleaning the rest room. Many people moreover do not much like the idea of cleaning the rest room for apparent reasons. However, you have not a few different desire due to the reality your lavatory will stink and you also do not need to sit down down on a grimy rest room. To clean the relaxation room, you need to begin with the flush address to save you germs from spreading. Wash and rinse the outdoors of the bathroom, the rest room seat, the bottom, the bottom and the lid. , pour a few disinfectant or bleach to sanitize. This will make it much less tough so you can put off stains and dust using your brush. Leave it for a couple of minutes in advance than brushing and rinsing.

Clean the bathe

You want to spray cleansing product at the bathe head and on the partitions and depart it for a couple of minutes in advance than scrubbing along side your brush. You must pick out out a purifier this is specifically made for placing off cleaning cleansing cleaning soap scum, green and rust-coloured stains, lime, rust, and calcium buildup. You can find out this information on the identical time as you look at the label at the back of the product. You can also soak the showerhead in vinegar and water combination overnight after disposing of it if it has too much cleansing soap scum or tough water buildup.

After soaking, easy the showerhead using a toothbrush to make it look colorful as new. Rinse the bathe vicinity very well with heat water and dry with a paper towel. For the shower floor, do not use an abrasive or metallic wool because it may harm the floor. Just use a broom with soft bristles to put off dust.

You also need to update your shower curtain specially if it has mildew and mildew. You can smooth your dirty bathe curtain thru washing it in warmness water with cleaning soap and bleach. You also can spray the moldy regions with bleach and water answer.

Clean the tub

When cleaning a porcelain tub, you need to use liquid cleanser or nonabrasive powder. You can use a gentle sponger for areas that aren't dirty and a scouring pad to eliminate hard stains and dust. For discolored porcelain, you may combo collectively cream of tartar and hydrogen peroxide or borax and lemon juice to create a paste which you can use to clean the stain at the porcelain. Just take a look at the paste at the stained area, go away it for a few minutes, scrub, and rinse thoroughly.

For rust stains, you could find out a commercial purifier that mainly gets rid of stains from rust. Just ensure which you are sporting rubber gloves due to the fact those cleaners encompass acid. If your bathtub is manufactured from fiberglass, you need to use a unique cleaning product that is mainly used for this type of material. You ought to moreover cast off the hairs that get caught inside the drain to save you it from clogging.

Clean the sink and countertop

You can dispose of cleaning soap scum and toothpaste from the sink using a everyday cleaner. To get to those tough to gain places round your tap, you can use an vintage toothbrush or cotton swabs. Never easy your sink and countertop using the identical sponger or towel that you used for cleansing the toilet due to the truth germs may additionally spread on the sink and counter.

Chapter 6: Cleaning and Organizing your Kitchen

You have to moreover smooth your kitchen thoroughly because of the truth that is one a part of your home which can get sincerely dirty while not wiped smooth regularly. This is because the kitchen is the vicinity in that you put together food and wash grimy dishes. It might also have food debris, liquid spills, stains, oil, and other dirt that you want to easy proper away. Cleaning the kitchen can be the most tough a part of own family cleansing and organizing due to the numerous kitchen appliances that you need to easy. Here are a few useful suggestions and techniques for cleaning your kitchen.

Cleaning kitchen home device

You need to smooth your kitchen appliances in advance than you smooth the room itself. Here are a few kitchen domestic device that require cleansing.

•   Stove. You want to smooth the burners whether or not or not you are the usage of a fuel or electric powered powered range. These can be eliminated and cleaned the use of warmth water with cleansing soap. You can both wash them with the aid of hand or the use of a dishwasher depending at the kind of burner you have. To eliminate oil splatter and meals particles from the floor of the variety, use a mild sponge soaked in soapy water. As a famous rule, you need to easy any oil spill and grease proper away to prevent them from staining the range floor and from collecting which makes it even more difficult to smooth.

You also can eliminate the knobs and wash them in warm soapy water. The vent hood want to also be cleaned often by way of the use of putting off the filters and soaking them in warmth soapy water. For the outdoors part of the vent hood, use a wet material with cleansing soap and wipe with easy damp fabric earlier than wiping it dry.

•   Oven. Aside from the range, you furthermore can also moreover want to smooth your oven very well. Take out the grates and soak them in a massive basin or bucket with warmth soapy water for numerous hours. This will make the grease and food debris mild which makes them less difficult to scrub off using a scouring pad. Electric ovens also have the cleansing mode desire which you could use to clean the oven. You need to wipe off any leftover dirt and residue with a moist fabric once the cycle is over.

You can smooth a fuel oven manually using a home made cleansing combination made from baking soda, salt, and water. Apply this combination at the internal ground of the oven and depart in a unmarried day. Be nice to cowl the clog openings and bare metals with aluminum foil to guard them from the combination. The subsequent day, cast off the mixture from the floor the usage of a plastic spatula then wipe it off with a easy rag. Put the racks decrease lower back in as speedy as they are dry.

• Refrigerator. The refrigerator want to be wiped easy once in a while. Remove all of the contents of the refrigerator and make certain which you throw away any leftover that you could not devour or any food object that has already expired. To clean the internal surfaces and the detachable parts inclusive of the racks, containers, and cabinets of the fridge, dip a sponge in a combination of baking soda and water.

Scrub off any sticky stains as a result of spills. Wipe off any residue using a clean damp cloth. One tip to save you awful smells internal your refrigerator is to move away an opened area of baking soda inside the fridge. Charcoals also have the same effect however they may get messy. You should additionally cover your leftover food to incorporate their smells.

• Freezer. If you have got were given a separate freezer, you must also defrost it often to make certain that it is taking walks effectively. Remove the frozen gadgets from the freezer and positioned them in a cooler for the meantime. You can prepare a domestic made solution the use of water, vinegar, and dish cleaning cleaning soap and pour the solution in a spray bottle. Spray the insides of the freezer collectively collectively together with your answer, wipe off with paper towels, and positioned the frozen items decrease back into the freezer.

If you still have the manual of your kitchen home gadget, you could take a look at the commands on cleaning the gadget particularly the ones small kitchen appliances like microwave, toaster, waffle maker, deep fryer, and so forth.

Clean and de-litter counters and cabinets

Your shelves might also additionally shop diverse matters collectively with food objects, spices, cleansing factors, dishes, small kitchen domestic system, and masses of greater. Throw away meals gadgets which is probably already expired, kitchen home tool which can be beyond restore, and plates and glasses which is probably broken. These are honestly taking over area to your shelves which you may use for storing extra useful subjects.

To de-litter your counter, you need to maintain your small home system indoors shelves or on pinnacle of them. This manner, you may have greater loose counter area that you could use for cooking and getting prepared food. This may additionally maintain your countertop from looking cluttered. If you've got were given a small kitchen and you have not any desire however to vicinity your small kitchen domestic gadget at the counter, you ought to as a minimum cover them with uniform cloth covers to guard them from dirt and to cause them to look fascinating to the eyes.

It is simple to smooth the cabinets. Just get a wet rag or material and wipe the surface and insides to get rid of dirt, crumbs, and dirt particles. You need to moreover wipe the counter the usage of a moist sponge soaked in soapy water. Wipe dry with paper towels or easy dish rags. Ideally, you must easy your countertop each day after cooking or getting prepared meals.

Clean the sink

The first difficulty that you need to do is to smooth all the grimy dishes in advance than cleaning the sink. Using a sponge and dish cleaning soap, wash the basin and the faucet to take away any cleaning soap scum, water stains, and meals debris. If your faucet water has immoderate mineral content cloth, you will see a buildup of mineral deposits. You can cast off this thru definitely blending collectively equal factors of water and white vinegar. Soak a dish rag into the answer and wipe off the mineral deposit buildup. Rinse with easy water.

You additionally need to make certain that your garbage disposal is strolling nicely because of the fact this may clog up your sink drainage. You need to recollect jogging the rubbish disposal if water does now not bypass down the sink drainage as speedy as it must. You must clean your garbage disposal occasionally through way of freezing vinegar in ice cube trays and dropping the frozen vinegar cubes into the disposal. While the disposal is jogging, pour boiling water to clean and sharpen the blades.

Clean the ground

Before you do any deep cleansing, you have to sweep up dirt, small quantities of trash, crumbs, and one of a kind element that you could take away the use of a brush and a dustpan. You must deep easy the floor specially if there are stains and spills and sticky food residue. You can use a mop dipped in soapy water for thorough ground cleaning.

Chapter 7: Cleaning and Organizing your Living Room

The residing room might be one of the most effective rooms of the residence to smooth. This will top notch require some dusting, wiping, vacuuming, and mopping. However, it is despite the fact that essential to make sure that you are cleaning the space very well due to the reality that is wherein you and your family typically maintain close out at the same time as you're at domestic. This is likewise the vicinity in which you entertain guests and it'd be a disgrace if the living room appears dirty and unkempt. Here are a few useful hints and strategies for cleaning and organizing the living room.

Get rid of dirt

The first aspect which you need to do is to dust the ceiling using a plastic broom. If your residing room has a excessive ceiling, you may want to apply a ladder however be cautious. You furthermore need to dust lighting fixtures together with chandeliers and overhead lights. For this, you need to no longer use a broom because it will not be capable of gain the small nooks and crannies of these lighting. You ought to use a duster with extendable address for the ones lighting installation immoderate up in the ceiling. You have to then dirt artwork, snap shots, lamp, vases, and exclusive suggests. You can use a microfiber cloth to wipe the floor of the coffee table, aspect tables, and cabinets.

Straighten out matters inside the dwelling room

To straighten out the living room, you need to get rid of factors that don't belong there. You need to additionally positioned yet again subjects in their respective places - positioned lower returned the books in the e-book shelf, set up the DVDs and CDs properly and located them decrease back within the CD rack, and so forth. You must moreover reposition sofa cushions so that they put on gently, straighten rugs that are not within the right function, fold throw rugs and Afghans, and so forth. If the whole lot is in the proper location, your dwelling room will right now appearance neat and tidy.

Wipe off the surfaces

You can use a moist rag to wipe the table pinnacle, home windows, TV and different digital home device, or maybe the patio door. Do not soak the rug due to the fact this can harm your timber furniture and electronic domestic equipment. If you could easy the furniture the usage of a duster or dry fabric, you need to pass using the moist fabric altogether.

Spot easy stains

If your carpet, rug, or upholstery has stains, you want to take into account doing spot cleaning. Spot cleaning allows you to awareness your energy and interest on the stain. This technique is a exceptional time saver due to the truth you're focusing at the vicinity that has a stain. You can use slight detergent and a wet fabric and rub it quick on the stained region.

Clean the couch

You want to clean the couch with the aid of vacuuming all of the nook and crannies. You may be amazed at the topics that you discover after cleaning the sofa. Rearrange the cushions in order that they get even placed on and tear. Finally, change the covers of the throw pillows and rearrange them nicely.

Clean the house domestic windows

You can spray glass purifier on the window and wipe it off with a newspaper. You also can use dishwashing detergent and a squeegee to make the windows smooth and easy. If you have were given builtin drapes, bear in mind vacuuming or dry cleansing them. If you have got were given regular curtains, you may update them with clean curtains that fit the room's colour motif.

Disinfect the an extended manner flung controls and phone

The mobile phone, far off controls, and online game controllers lure germs due to the fact there are some of the things which you keep almost each day. You want to sanitize those objects for your dwelling room using a disinfecting wipe. Many human beings overlook approximately the ones objects but they didn't apprehend that those are in fact some of the dirtiest gadgets in the living room.

Clean the ground

Vacuum the rugs and carpet to get rid of dirt, hair, and notable small debris. Be certain to vacuum beneath the sofa and inside the lower back of the TV cupboard. If you have were given a tiled or marbled floor, you can continuously use a wet mop to deep smooth the ground.

Add greater garage devices

You need to do not forget which include extra garage gadgets for your residing room specifically when you have kids. After playing inside the residing room, they might located their toys in boxes that also double as ottomans. By adding greater garage devices, you're minimizing the litter that could make your living room look untidy.

Clean adjacent rooms

After cleaning the residing room, you need to additionally recall cleaning the adjoining rooms which incorporates the lobby or hallway. These regions do not clearly have hundreds of factors in them. You simply want to hoover the floor and dirt off the wall art work and other indicates. People generally grasp their coat, leave their dirty shoes, and go away their umbrellas in the foyer. Make tremendous which you moreover smooth the foyer very well specifically at some point of wet days. Your lobby need to have a coat hanger, a basket for umbrellas, and a shoe rack for grimy footwear.

Chapter 8: Cleaning and Organizing your Dining Room

Cleaning and organizing the eating room is a bit like cleansing and organizing your dwelling room and kitchen. This is as it additionally has decors and furnishings much like the residing room however it has the same shape of dust determined in the kitchen, despite the reality that the kitchen can be dirtier. You want to easy and prepare your ingesting room very well due to the reality this is in that you and your circle of relatives devour and this is moreover in that you from time to time entertain guests on the equal time as you invite them over for dinner.

De-muddle your consuming room

Get rid of things that need to be in wonderful rooms like newspapers, magazines, dirty cups and plates, toys, and so on. Once those are removed, you have to additionally put together the subjects which is probably on display on your cupboard which includes collectible collectible figurines, vases, or excellent china. Although having a show cabinet isn't always clearly vital in a ingesting room, it is despite the fact that first rate to get one particularly if you have best porcelain china and dinnerware to show. You do no longer want your children or pets to via the usage of danger stumble upon the show and break them into tiny portions. You need to choose a show cabinet with glass doors so that the exquisite china and collectible collectible figurines are included from dust.

Get rid of dust

Just like in a few different rooms, you need to begin from the ceiling in advance than you flow directly to the walls and sooner or later to the ground. Remove the dust from the ceiling and partitions the usage of a brush or feather duster. You want to additionally get rid of the dirt on the ground of the show cabinets and on the eating room desk.

Clean the eating table and chairs

Aside from dusting, you need to additionally learn how to eliminate stains and water marks from our ingesting desk. This is a commonplace trouble in case you are the use of a wood table. This is why it is crucial to apply a placemat or a coaster whilst eating to save you any stains and marks from unfavourable your table. If your dining chairs are upholstered, you must spot easy any stains because of liquid spills and food particles. You can guard your consuming chairs using a seat cowl.

Clean the floor

Once you have got wiped smooth and organized the ceiling, partitions, paintings, cabinet, shows, consuming table, and ingesting chair, you need to now begin cleaning the ground. You can sweep the ground first to take away dust and dust particles earlier than vacuuming. Vacuuming is critical in particular if your ingesting room floors have a wall to wall carpet. If you have were given timber or marbled floors, you may smooth it thoroughly using a mop.

Chapter 9: Cleaning and Organizing the Garage and Patio

The storage and patio also are a part of your home however they may be especially considered grow to be independent from the possibility rooms. Most human beings use the garage for storage at the same time as others renovate their storage and turn it right right into a activity room or an prolonged residing area. The patio is taken into consideration an prolonged a part of the dwelling room because it serves the same motive due to the fact the residing room. The simplest difference is that the patio is considered outdoor. Here are some important guidelines and worries for cleaning and organizing the garage and patio.

Organizing the storage

The storage is one of the maximum tough areas of your property to prepare due to the wide range of factors saved in it. Your organizational competencies may be positioned to the check when organizing the garage. The most crucial factor that you need to do is to corporation similar topics collectively like gardening factors, car gear and elements, poison and toxic chemical substances, sports sports and out of doors machine, doggy sources, and so forth. You can assign powerful areas inside the garage in which you can set up your stuff in line with the sorts that you have come up with. Write the name of the class on a chunk of cardboard or timber and hand it on the wall so you apprehend in which to transport when you are looking for a few issue.

You want to shop for severa sorts of storage gadgets collectively with steel cabinets, bike racks, cabinets, and bins to help you set up your stuff results. You can also take gain of the wall or ceiling. You can cling your bike or surfboards on the wall or you can draw close them on the ceiling in case your storage has a immoderate ceiling and you aren't using it to park your automobile. You can maintain small knick knacks in conjunction with Christmas ornaments in plastic bins to shield them from dust and dust.

The appropriate issue approximately organizing your storage is that you can find out masses of factors to promote. These are topics that you no longer want or want but are nevertheless in appropriate state of affairs. You can sell them on-line or you can preserve a garage sale within the the front of your house.

Cleaning the storage

Cleaning the garage can take plenty of time so make sure to time table a whole weekend most effective for this reason. You do now not really want to clean it very well the way you'll your mattress room or lavatory due to the truth that is in which you park your automobile and keep wonderful styles of components. To easy the storage, in reality type through your things and throw away matters that you now not need or aren't usable which include dried paint, broken sports sports equipment, and so on. You need to smooth the storage one vicinity at a time to keep your self from feeling too beaten with all the stuff which you need to kind out. Remove dust and cobwebs using a brush with lengthy cope with and sweep the floor the usage of the equal broom.

Cleaning the patio

The patio is difficult to clean up due to the truth it's miles taken into consideration an outside region but it has furniture portions, however the fact that the fixtures quantities are mainly made for outdoor use. Your essential problems are mould, bleaching, and dust. You can scrub off the mould the use of a sponge soaked in warmth soapy water. To convey once more the colour of your fixtures, recollect repainting or refinishing them. Bleaching is due to extended publicity to daylight hours. This can be avoided in case you role your furniture on this form of manner that they'll be now not exposed to direct daylight hours or you can cover them speedy at the same time as no longer in use. You also can easy the cushions using the equal sponge and warmth soapy water. To put off dust and dirt that get caught in crevices and wheels, you could use an vintage toothbrush and soapy water.

Aside from the fixtures, you moreover mght want to smooth different subjects that belong within the patio which consist of the barbecue grill. To degrease the grill, flip it on for about ten mins to melt the residue that coats the grill. Turn off the grill and scrape off the softened dust the usage of a cord brush or a crumpled ball of aluminum foil, making sure no longer to touch the ultra-modern grill. When the grill isn't heat to the touch, you may take out the grease tray and soak it in warm soapy water earlier than washing and rinsing. Put the tray lower again in the grill at the same time as you are achieved cleansing it, flip off the propane tank, and cover the grill for subsequent use.

To smooth the floor of the patio, you may use a strain washing system to put off any dirt and soil debris that gets stuck in among the wooden floors.

Organize the patio

Organizing the patio is straightforward due to the reality there are not too many stuff that you could find out on this part of your house. You can be innovative with garage via deciding on something that resultseasily blends within the surrounding. For example, you may pick out out an antique chest that seems like a treasure chest in which you may keep blankets for those cool nights, more candles, and so forth.

Chapter 10: Hold a Yard Sale

After cleansing and organizing the residence, you have got were given in all likelihood accrued pretty some stuff which might be nevertheless in extremely good circumstance but you not need or want. To grow to be the remaining spouse that every woman desires to be, you must additionally remember methods to earn coins at the facet. And what better way to earn cash than to sell the litter in your private home with the aid of using manner of shielding a outdoor sale? You are de-cluttering your house and on the equal time being profitable from it. You can look at the hints underneath if you are making plans to preserve a outside sale.

Gather all the gadgets

You must collect all the gadgets that you have collected in the special rooms of your private home in some unspecified time in the future of the clean up. Put them in containers to make it much less complex so that you can bring them outdoor. The things which may be most generally offered in storage earnings are vintage clothes, toys, books, collectibles, pastimes, vintage furniture, CDs, and electronics, to listing down some. Do no longer revel in unhappy which you are parting techniques with these items that you have had for years. After all, you haven't been the use of them for pretty some time now and also you likely wouldn't remember them when you have not finished a modern clean up.

Make a list of a number of the gadgets

Some humans do now not problem growing a list however it s important to list down the topics which you are making plans to sell and their corresponding charges. You may additionally additionally want to research the current marketplace fees of positive gadgets particularly uncommon collectibles. It might be tough to provide you an low-cost rate instantaneous if the price tag gets lost and also you do not have a charge listing with you. Making an inventory list can be tedious however it ensures smoother transactions among you and your purchasers. You do not constantly need to down even the small items like your hundreds of romance books that price $0.25 each. Just consist of the ones big and steeply-priced gadgets for your list in particular the ones that require research to get the present day market rate.

Put a fee tag on each object

To save you clients from asking you the costs of the items over and over, you need to write down down the rate on an adhesive labels and stick it at the item on the market. If customers ask you strategies plenty a fantastic item is, just inform him that he can find out the rate in the connected tag. You can also use a masking tape if you do now not have a decal label.

Get the essential permit

Before you maintain a backyard sale, you need to first get a allow from the residence proprietor's association or from the town place of job. Some places are strict as regards to this stuff. They have rules consisting of the term that you may have the outdoor sale, the frequency, the location of the sign, and so on. On the alternative hand, there are towns and neighborhoods which might be more lenient but make sure to visit the house owner's association or ask your friends if a allow is wanted to preserve a outside sale.

Pick a date in your out of doors sale

You should pick a date whilst there are pretty some humans in your community, like in the path of summer season weekends. It is excellent to maintain a -

day sale to provide people a risk to return lower again and bring pals with them. The longer the exposure, the greater income you may have. You ought to additionally test the climate forecast. You do now not want your matters to get soaked inside the rain honestly because you failed to check the weather forecast on the date of your backyard sale. You must additionally keep away from setting your outside sale date on a holiday or even as there's a very unique occasion because of the fact humans most in all likelihood have other more crucial sports and locations to be than to go to a yard sale.

Advertise your backyard sale

You can promote it your backyard sale in your community newspaper or radio station to allow people understand about the event. You need to put up the commercial multiple days earlier than to provide human beings hundreds of time to encompass your event in their time table. If you market it the event weeks in advance, humans will maximum likely overlook approximately about it. Another way to promote it is to offer out flyers spherical your community and put up them in bulletin boards.

Take out your matters

Hours in advance than the sale, you have to take out your stuff so that after people arrive, the entirety which you are making plans to sell are already on display. You will want tables for some of your gadgets and you need boxes and baggage wherein your customers can placed their purchases. You want to moreover prepare small bills and change for even as your customers pay big payments.

Chapter 11: The Trouble with Cleaning

The charge of residing does now not seem to get any much less pricey, in truth, it seems to be on a very upward spiral. Even simple such things as cleansing your home can upload massive fees to the weekly or month-to-month payments. When it entails cleansing and coping with our homes the ones prices do not just increase to our economic group balances but also to the surroundings. Commercial cleaning products are not frequently environmentally first-rate and the few manufacturers which can be will be predisposed to price an extended way extra than large cleaning products.

If you would really like to find methods to reduce each the price of coping with your home and the hidden price to the surroundings, then this ebook can be for you. Cleaning and own family control hacks are easy techniques in which to keep money and time on domestic jobs and use materials which might be, for the maximum issue, heaps more consistent than traditional, commercially produced merchandise. The hints and hacks in this book aren't new; they were used for generations via the use of homemakers. In reality, most of them date again to a time on the equal time because the massive array of cleaning merchandise we discover on maintain shelves these days virtually didn't exist.

Modern Cleaning Products are Better, Right?

Well, no longer in reality. While contemporary merchandise and strategies are marketed as being green and fantastically powerful they may be no longer sincerely any higher than the own family hacks to be observed on this e-book. The hacks have, despite the whole lot, been employed for generations and feature stood the take a look at of time. More modern merchandise do paintings but they achieve this at a fee. It is within the hobbies of the producers of these products to suggest that present day-day cleaning products are better than conventional cleansing strategies and, of direction, they provide a excessive diploma of consolation for those parents with busy lives to influence.

The intention of this ebook is to help you find out strategies to easy and control your home, that have been used within the past, to lessen down the time you spend cleansing and, of path, to save you cash. There are clean hacks that may be applied in pretty a first-rate deal each problem of cleansing and coping with your home and this consists of the whole thing from maintaining furniture clean to drains easy from blockages.

Chemical Warfare

It's no accident that in recent terrorist threats number one, enterprise cleansing merchandise were used to create deadly guns. Most present day cleansing products are lethal and embody chemical materials which may be actually now not safe. For people with allergic reactions, youngsters and pets, the principle trouble is safety in phrases of this form of cleaning product. This e book takes that scenario notably and has looked at commonplace, traditional techniques which, with the useful aid of and big, avoid the usage of the greater risky chemical substances and materials that may be placed in mass produced cleaning merchandise.

Chemical stuffed cleaners can produce hypersensitive reactions and also can make gift ones masses worse. Many humans have already found out this and are keen to discover herbal, non-chemical tactics wherein to smooth their home. In this e-book the motive is that will help you discover loads less expensive, masses a great deal much less volatile techniques in which to preserve your property easy and manage it with out resorting to chemical conflict!

What Do I Need?

It's enormously probably that you could have plenty of the goods and substances said in this ebook already. Many may be decided to your kitchen cabinets and people which you need to stock up on need to show lots inexpensive than regular cleansing merchandise.

The materials that we check in this e-book embody:

• salt

• olive oil

• vegetable oil

- white vinegar

- baking soda

- citric acid

- washing soda

- dish washing liquid

- bleach

- hydrogen peroxide

Safety First

You'll phrase that some of those merchandise could in all likelihood fall into the class of 'chemical products' and it's far real that a number of them are the basic elements for extra complicated mass-produced merchandise. While many of the hacks use merchandise consisting of coarse salt and baking soda, every of which can be not likely to motive reactions and are not unstable in themselves, others, which incorporates bleach and hydrogen peroxide are extra unstable. Used successfully they will motive no damage or damage however it is vital to consider that some thing and everything that isn't steady to eat should be stored a long way from youngsters, especially very younger children, and pets.

Scentless Soaps

Natural and selfmade cleansing products do no longer consist of scents within the same manner that mass produced ones do. However you may, if you want, stock up on crucial oils to feature to many of the hacks and domestic made cleansing products we are going to be looking at. Where this is appropriate it's going to possibly be stated in the description of the technique or the recipe for you r new, extra healthy, greater regular and much less high-priced cleaning substances. Like the options that we may be exploring, essential oils are natural, safe and natural, so they may be regular to use in your property and no longer risky to the environment. Small portions of critical oils will move an extended manner and can be applied in a whole lot of precise cleansing hacks, so notwithstanding the fact that you could should make investments a bit in them, it will nonetheless be an exceptional investment and plenty less luxurious than the usage of mass produced cleansing merchandise. Where stated the necessities are not, however, critical to the recipe! So it's far surely non-obligatory as to whether you encompass them!

Chapter 12: Kitchen Cleaning Hacks

The kitchen is one of the busiest rooms in most houses and it's miles crucial to keep it easy and hygienic. It's in all likelihood one of the rooms in which we spend masses of our time cleaning and it's also one that charges the maximum in terms of cleansing products. So, what higher place to start exploring our Household Hacks?

Kitchen Wipes

Why purchase expensive cleaning wipes at the same time as you cause them to your self at a fraction of the cost? Simply break up antique garb, T-shirt cloth is great for this, into desired wipe sizes and drop them proper right into a jar. Mix in half of of a cup of water and half of of white vinegar and add critical oil to fragrance (your preference of oil). Place the top at the jar and supply it a notable shake to very well soak the rags, and that is it. Vinegar is a herbal disinfectant and this is manner to it's miles acidic nature. It kills off bugs and inactivates a few viruses (at the side of the flu virus). The rags, in comparison to enterprise wipes, also can be washed and re-used! For some jobs you may need to squeeze out a number of the excess liquid in advance than wiping.

Bacteria and Boards

Wooden decreasing forums are determined in maximum kitchens however are at risk of cuts and scratches through the years. Cleaning them very well is essential as it's far indoors those grooves and marks that bacteria can motel and thrive. A herbal and less costly manner to smooth them is to in reality sprinkle salt on the board and reduce a lemon in half (lime can also paintings nicely) and provide the board an amazing scrub with the lemon as though it have been a scrubbing brush. Lemon, like vinegar, has a excessive acid content material cloth and this lets in to clean and disinfect. The salt will help to do away with strains of meals and dirt. Once completed, wipe off any residue and rinse and dry as everyday.

Cleaning the Cleaners

If your dishwasher is in normal use then it is likely to need some easy, loving care every so often. The dishwasher takes the stress in many present day kitchens however all that cleaning can leave it in want of a first rate wash itself! A smooth, secure and non-poisonous way in which to clean it utilities baking soda and white vinegar. Run the dishwasher through it's miles everyday wash placing however place a cup of white vinegar on the pinnacle rack. Once this has completed, place a cup of baking soda on the pinnacle rack and run through some specific cycle. The vinegar will help to smooth via slicing thru grease and helping to get rid of micro organism whilst the Baking Soda rinse moreover cleans and deodorizes your device. You can do that as little as some times a three hundred and sixty five days, or as quickly as a month for incredible outcomes.

Victorian Cleaning Values

Ammonia is any such cleaning products that has been to be had for many years. Even our Victorian forebears ought to apprehend it and it is one of the few family cleaners that would had been to be had to them! It is one among many components that can be located in favored cleansing merchandise however it could but be offered as a stand-by myself purifier. It has many uses round the house and in the kitchen it without a doubt works a deal with for cleaning the burners, oven racks and grill racks from your range and grill. Place the burners in a single day in a bag with best a small amount of ammonia sprinkled over them. Ideally depart this in the sink, to avoid the risk of spillages. For grill or oven racks you can want a bag large sufficient to honestly encase them. Of the products used in this ebook, ammonia is one that want to continually be stored and used faraway from youngsters and animals. In the morning, actually rinse the burners and racks under warmth water and they'll be as ideal as new!

Coffee Pot Cleaning

When it entails preserving coffee pots easy you may find out that the chore is a common one. Coffee stains quick building up in our espresso makers but they need now not be a pain to easy. This method is a smooth, secure and natural approach and uses no longer whatever more than easy white vinegar. Simply upload more than one cups of white vinegar on your device and run it through a brewing cycle. Once completed depart the vinegar to face for approximately fifteen to 20 mins. After this time pour the vinegar away and run the cycle another time with just water – to dispose of any vinegar flavor!

Blitzing the Blender

Like our coffee pots and makers our blenders and food mixers are essential kitchen gadget. They're furthermore tough and time ingesting to easy. Not anymore! Simply upload a few heat water and a hint of sizeable detergent proper away after use. Blitz, empty and check no food has been left over, rinse and dry as everyday. This technique is speedy however moreover make sure that no linger scraps of meals can be left immediately to encourage bacterial growth.

Cast Iron Solutions

Cast iron pans are fantastic and are determined in most kitchens – often used very often. Cleaning merchandise are not, but, constantly the fine for them as they're capable of rapid harm the pans, shortening their lifespan and could usually eliminate the protective layer of oil that keeps the pans in their fantastic circumstance. A secure and natural opportunity cleansing method is honestly to apply coarse salt to scrub your solid iron cookware with. Once the pan, or skillet, is clean surely wipe off any extra salt and rub in a touch clean oil to help hold the pan's "seasoning". This approach isn't always excellent higher for your pans but an extended manner much less steeply-priced than business cleaning fluids.

Pesky Pesticides

Chemicals can be found in use in all regions of our lives and our food isn't any exception. Pesticides utilized in farming often live on our clean fruit and veggies and, regardless of the truth that typically harmless in tiny doses, no character without a doubt likes the concept of eating them! While washing and cleaning your greens in water will remove a number of the dirt and lingering chemicals, many humans favor to use a representative vegetable washing liquid. The less expensive possibility is to supply your non-public, of route! For this you could want to stock up on some Hydrogen Peroxide. This useful addition on your cleaning cabinet has a variety of makes use of and we're going to be assembly it once more later inside the ebook. For cleaning functions you should buy the 3% range (pharmaceutical grade). Simply upload ¼ cup to a sink entire of water and wash your greens as everyday. Rinse very well with water as soon because the greens have been wiped clean.

Ice Box Answers

Who loves cleaning out the refrigerator? If you are one of the few that do, then you definately definately sincerely could probably want to bypass this step. For the rest of us, cleansing the fridge is a pain. To make the chore much less complicated clearly line your refrigerator with plastic location-mats or kitchen tissues. Place-mats are the extremely good choice, easy to take away, wipe and go back to the fridge. They capture spills and stray meals and assist to make cleaning out the refrigerator (nearly) a pride. Add a small pot of baking soda within the back of the fridge to assist take in unpleasant smells. Baking soda is a natural deodorizer and will maintain your fridge smelling fresh.

Microwave Magic

Wiping, scrubbing and scouring all take their toll on one vital set of gadgets inside the kitchen; our wipes, scrubs, scourers and sponges. Bacteria may additionally moreover quick increase on these add-ons and so it's miles important to ensure that they'll be thoroughly wiped clean. The most effective way, and one of the oldest, is to use boiling water. This naturally sterilizes the cloths. A clean and charge effective way to do this is to use the microwave; honestly vicinity your cloth or sponge in a bowl of water and boil within the microwave for a few minutes, ideally clearly in advance than the usage of the fabric or sponge.

Hob Cleaning with the Hassle

Ceramic range tops appearance high-quality but they will be challenge to hundreds of harm and tear. Keeping them searching exceptional is quite simple however often costly, as they require especially designed cleaning lotions. Or do they? Well a cheap, however very effective, possibility involves the vintage favored baking soda. Sprinkle the top with the soda after which wet a huge cloth (or severa - sufficient to cover the pinnacle) in warmth, soapy water. Lay this on the baking soda and depart for amongst ten and twenty mins. Remove, wipe and buff. You'll be amazed!

Stainless and Scratch-much less Solutions

Stainless metallic fixtures and fittings are superb however they may be difficult to preserve looking their excellent. Rather than use high-priced cleaners (as with the oven) you may use baking soda. Baking soda cleans and deodorizes however it is also a mildly abrasive – so mild that it'll now not harm chrome steel in any respect. Use approximately three tablespoons jumbled collectively most effective a bit water and wipe over surfaces and sinks to get an in depth smooth. Wipe and rinse afterwards to do away with any residue. Baking soda is natural and secure, making it the right non-toxic and genuinely reasonably-priced alternative.

Time for a Grilling

If you're lucky enough to have a Foreman-fashion electric powered powered grill you will be extremely keen on it. Except, in terms of cleaning! However, this does not should be a time ingesting, messy or difficult assignment. When you have got got used the grill genuinely place some damp paper towels into the grill, ensuring that it is off, and near the grill. You can go away the towels in whilst you eat after which remove them and wipe down. Dirt, grease and meals scraps will all be prolonged past.

Chapter 13: Brighter Bathroom Hacks

Perhaps the subsequent room in our houses that sees the maximum traffic is the rest room. Keeping this room clean and glowing is virtually as difficult because of the truth the kitchen and, over again, it's miles a room in which we're able to spend hundreds of money and time within the try to accumulate this. In this monetary wreck we are able to take a look at simply how you can cut the charge and the quantity of time you need to spend cleansing the bathroom.

Toilet Issues

Stubborn stains inside the rest room bowl are unpleasant and embarrassing. Cleaning them is pricey and the chemical substances we use aren't the outstanding for the surroundings. One a whole lot less expensive, a great deal less tough and more steady way to preserve a glowing, easy lavatory bowl is to use Coke. Yes, the clean-drink this is additionally a (little recognized) miracle cleaner. Pour a bottle of coke, dousing the rim as you accomplish that, into the bowl and depart it to sit for at least an hour. Flush the coke away and you may find out that maximum cussed stains will go with it.

Banishing Odors

Baking soda is, once more, extraordinarily beneficial in the rest room. Simply keep a pot of it near, or in the back of, the relaxation room to maintain any unsightly smells at bay. You ought to update it often, certainly flush it down the toilet and it's going to help to provide the drains a hint freshen as it goes!

Natural Scents

The floor across the relaxation room in masses of houses is treated with some disrespect. If you maintain guys or boys in your own family you may be properly privy to what we imply! To get rid of the "natural" scents they go away at the back of you can find out that a baking soda mixture will art work in addition to any business cleaner. Mix baking soda with lemon juice, to a thick paste, and exercise to the affected location round the rest room. Leave the aggregate for fifteen to twenty minutes earlier than spraying with white vinegar. The aggregate will froth and depart it until it has stopped foaming. Next use a humid material to treatment the residue. Apply as soon as a month or as required.

Nicer Natural Scents

If you need extra scents in your lavatory, neglect industrial air fresheners and sprinkle a touch vital oil of your choice throughout the room. You should buy a small oil burner to preserve the air freshly scented. Essential oils are less expensive and could final longer and, in mixture together together with your baking soda deodorizer will assist to preserve unsightly odors properly and virtually at bay.

Pampering Porcelain

Bathroom porcelain, collectively with the sink and relaxation room have a take a look at their first-rate whilst they'll be clean and remarkable. Using steeply-priced porcelain polishes is one technique to acquire this affect however the usage of Baby Oil is absolutely as powerful and far much less costly! You'll only want a drop or two on a fabric to polish to a super shine. Only use this hack at the sinks and rest room bowls – it isn't appropriate for the bathtub bathtub. Polish until the porcelain feels dry and shines as brightly as possible.

Natural Cleaning Spray

To easy your bathtub you may make your non-public, herbal, stable and price effective rest room cleaning spray. In a bowl, or pouring jug, mixture up ¾ of a cup of baking soda, three tablespoons of salt, ½ cup of white vinegar and three tablespoons of dishwasher detergent. For fragrance upload a few drops of your chosen critical oil, however the truth that this isn't always required. Pour the aggregate into a spray bottle and supply it an splendid shake earlier than use. Use as you will a everyday bathtub cleaning spray. The spray might also even paintings on tiles, just as efficaciously as any you can buy within the shops!

Safe Scouring

To offer your bathtub tub an extremely good scrub use baking soda. A herbal, but mild, scouring substance baking soda want to be safe to apply on any shape of bath. Mix one cup of soda with a bit water or liquid cleaning cleansing soap to make a thick paste, observe with a sponge or damp fabric and rinse as normal. This is a quite effective way to clean the bath and it's very environmentally high-quality.

Sherbet Shower Head Cleaner

Over a remarkably quick time bathe heads can emerge as grimy, grimy and clogged with lime-scale and residue. While industrial cleaning merchandise will supply them lower again to their former glory, right antique baking soda and white vinegar will do the identical at a fraction of the fee and certainly as effectively. For this hack you'll want a huge, sturdy plastic bag. Add a hint baking soda and sufficient white vinegar to immerse the whole shower head. If you're brave you could do this with shower head in location – be cautious to connect the bag securely. If it's far feasible to get rid of the bathe head this can be the more stable/much less hard choice. The combination will fizz away merrily and need to be left to artwork its magic for more than one hours, overnight for fine effects. Simply wipe, or rinse, the bathe head in heat water and it is going to be fairly clean over again.

Mold and Mildew Defense

Plastic shower curtains additionally may be tough gadgets to hold clean. Thanks to the combination of warmth and moisture within the rest room, mould can form in all varieties of locations, together with on the bathe curtain. Prevention is the first rate step in this case; soak a new curtain in warmth water (in the bath is proper) with ¼ cup of family salt. Leave for 3 to four hours, or overnight if feasible, after which get rid of. The salt creates a natural, shielding barrier which will prevent mildew from forming. You can repeat at everyday periods to lengthen the impact.

Mold in the rest room is unsightly but it is also a health risk. Thanks to the weather in maximum bathrooms it's miles, but, a commonplace problem. Heat and moisture integrate to make the correct breeding floor for this unpleasant increase. To reduce the risk of it developing, attempt to make certain that the bathroom fan runs whilst moisture and steam are gift but to take away it you'll want to spray with a solution of water and bleach. Mix up your spray with 10% bleach and 90% warm water. More bleach will don't have any more effect so do no longer use too much. Simply spray on and go away for ten mins or so earlier than wiping off with a moist cloth and then drying suddenly. A hair dryer is a splendid desire to get the vicinity dry speedy.

De-Misted Mirrors

Bathroom mirrors present a specific undertaking; they have a tendency to fog up simply whilst you want them maximum! There are severa strategies to save you this and all may be completed brief and affordably. The most commonplace are;

• Shaving foam. Simply wipe the replicate with foam and then towel down. This must keep the mirror from fogging up for several weeks.

• White Vinegar. Mix an answer of white vinegar and water (1/2 of and 1/2) in a twig bottle. Spray a first-rate mist onto the reflect and then wipe off. You can upload important oil, if required and wipe off with vintage newspaper to reduce streaks as well as fog. This want to last for severa days at least.

• Dish cleansing cleaning soap, or preferred washing liquid, may additionally moreover in reality have the same effect. Just wipe the mirror with a hint of cleaning cleaning cleaning soap and wipe easy. This will closing for approximately 24 hours.

- If you have got were given forgotten to use any of the above truely dry the reflect with a hair dryer to remove steam and fog proper now. Then use one of the above strategies for subsequent time!

Painful Stains

Stain removal is a ache. In the relaxation room cans, bottles and pots can leave stains within the relaxation room shelves or on surfaces. Rather than spend hours removing them, prevent them inside the first location via the usage of a easy nail polish to coat the lowest of them. Stains? What stains?

Delicate Disks

Deodorizing disks are wonderful but there can be no want to buy them at the store as you may make as many as you like at domestic! You also can, via now, be unsurprised to find that the fundamental problem is baking soda! In addition you can want a few boiling water, a muffin pan and essential oil to create a perfume. Popular scents include lemon, lime, lavender or rose, however the choice is yours. Simply aggregate two cups of baking soda with one cup of boiled water and ten drops of crucial oil collectively. Spoon into the muffin molds and leave till dry – it want to take among 24 and forty eight hours. Place the disks anywhere you require and they should be powerful for as a minimum a month.

Chapter 14: Living Room Hacks

Living rooms gift their very non-public problems with regards to cleansing. Spills, stains, scratches and smells all create hundreds of tough paintings for us. In this chapter we are going to take a look at reducing that paintings and furthermore the manner to keep your dwelling rooms searching smooth and cared for.

Leather Repair

Leather fixtures is outstanding because it's easy to wipe smooth. Useful if you have small children, animals or men inside the residence! However it does scratch effortlessly and this makes the furnishings regarded worn-out and antique earlier than its time. You can purchase (high-priced) leather-based care polishes to rectify the problem or you could use the on your fee range opportunity; the common-or-garden shoe polish. Simply find out the proper coloration to suit your furniture and polish and buff. To ensure the polish is dried and set, buff with a fabric till this comes away smooth — clothes will then be secure and your leather-based-primarily based-primarily based fixtures will appearance as top as new!

Scratch Mark Solutions

Wooden and plastic furnishings additionally may be difficulty to scratch marks and scrapes. A easy approach to revitalize the furnishings is to apply a everlasting marker pen. Some producers even manufacture professional pens for this cause but you can discover that for timber furniture it is easy to find out a match from the identical antique variety. It's a quick and powerful way to repair the coolest appears of scratched and damaged fixtures.

Natural Carpet Cleaning

There are hundreds of carpet cleaning and deodorizing products to be had in the market. However, they may be hardly ever cheap and a few human beings can also moreover find out that they've an hypersensitive reaction to them. There are herbal options, one in every of that is baking soda (yes, you guessed) and the alternative is cornstarch. Sprinkle both of those dry over the carpet and leave for an hour, earlier than vacuuming as everyday. This technique moreover may be used on upholstery to help do away with smells and maintain it glowing. Again, in fact sprinkle over the fixtures and go away for at least an hour in advance than vacuuming.

Get Glass Gleaming

Glass surfaces, such as espresso tables, domestic windows, cabinets and bookshelves are top notch, however they display dirt and marks right away. There is, but, no need for high priced sprays and cloths. Clean glass with warm temperature, slightly soapy water and dry and buff using vintage newspaper. Buffing with newspaper is a very antique technique and works as well as any contemporary (luxurious) opportunity. You can upload a bit white vinegar to the water to prevent streaks if you choice.

Stubborn Stains

Especially for people with babies or pets there are a few stains which we would as an opportunity forget about. Vomit, urine and mucus all find out their manner onto our upholstery and carpets. To easy vomit stains from furniture combination up a paste of baking soda and water, make sure the paste is pretty thick and practice to the affected place. Leave for eight to 12 hours, thru which era the baking soda want to be dry once more. Vacuum multiple times to do away with the baking soda and the stain.

For stains on carpets a solution of water, white vinegar and baking soda is wanted. Mix cups of white vinegar with of heat water and upload 4 tablespoons of baking soda. You can mixture this in a sprig bottle and exercise to the affected region; depart for five to ten mins and the use a towel to get rid of the combination. Repeat if essential and sprinkle the region with baking soda preceding to vacuuming to make sure any residual heady scent is eliminated.

Chapter 15: Laundry Hacks

The laundry room, or honestly your washing device, are at the coronary coronary heart of the circle of relatives cleansing regime. As properly as keeping your house easy you'll spend some of time cleansing clothes. As with all different regions of domestic cleansing this may display to be a highly-priced challenge. Basic cleaning merchandise aren't high priced however preserving all of your clothes, bedding, throws and fabrics in their exceptional circumstance can suggest shopping for a number of cleansing products, softeners and conditioners. Some fabric are more difficult to smooth than others and even as everything is taken into consideration laundry might not be rocket generation, but it comes near! In this economic ruin we will take a look at some hacks you can set up on the same time as doing the laundry and whilst organizing your everyday. These need to assist to maintain this crucial characteristic of home art work on foot smoothly, decreasing the time you spend on it and the fee for your rate range.

How Clean is Your Washing Machine?

Washing machines collect dirt and dust; this is their manner in spite of the whole lot. However, over the years this builds up and, of path, lessens the effectiveness of every wash. If you've got a large circle of relatives and the machine seems to be in ordinary use this will take location exceedingly brief. Keeping your device glowing and smooth will assist to make sure that every wash works to it is quality impact. To deliver it a short and easy freshen, run it on a warmness cycle with a teaspoon of baking soda and multiple teaspoons of white vinegar. As it virtually works it is manner via the device the solution cleans and deodorizers. You can try this as often as you observe in form but as quickly as a month or so need to be loads.

The Sock Monster

As with the Loch Ness Monster, rumors of this creature's lifestyles have circulated for years. Odd socks frequently seem inside the laundry and may take months to healthy up with their missing partner. Hang a line on your laundry room, a bit of string will do, and clip those lonesome creatures on as you find them. Soon you may discover their lacking contrary numbers and you may reunite them. If not for correct, at the least for now.

Sensitive Stain Busters

Stains on apparel are to be had all sizes and styles and they may lessen the lifespan of your garb notably. You can inventory up on pricey stain removers, which also can do greater damage in your clothes inside the long term, or you may try the following easy (much less high priced) and fast performing hacks.

• Hair spray; actual old skool hair spray is an powerful stain remover in an emergency. Simply spray without delay to the stain and allow artwork for twenty to thirty mins. Blot the stain with a moist fabric to dispose of. This works properly on most solvent stains, which consist of lipstick.

Chapter 16: General Cleaning Tips and Tricks

So, we've got got were given the kitchen included, the laundry laid out, the dwelling room re-booted and the rest room lovely. However, there are though some own family hacks that you may employ anywhere within the residence (and past) to make your lifestyles much less complicated, cheaper and greater inexperienced. In this very last bankruptcy we are going to test a few clean but effective modern-day-day own family guidelines.

Cleaning Regimes

This may additionally moreover sound easy but it is pretty effective for reducing down the time it takes to clean your property. There are essential methods to hire; easy little and regularly and write a cleaning listing.

Firstly, the little and frequently technique manner making smooth cleaning duties part of specific sporting activities. Pour that bottle of coke down the relaxation room within the morning while certainly everybody has completed with the room. Wipe spherical the sink within the kitchen and relaxation room final trouble at night time. This keeps subjects in pinnacle order and technique "large cleans" are much less time-ingesting.

For those big cleans have a listing of chores and obligations. How regularly have you ever observed your self starting one method, being interrupted by means of manner of the use of every other, and so on? Simply have a cleaning plan and stay with it. Organize your plan thru room and set up chores in a practical way (go away mopping kitchens until ultimate on the kitchen listing, and so forth.).

House Rules

Shoes and homes do now not blend! Make this a clean rule to your circle of relatives; at least 70% of the dirt that comes into our homes comes in at the soles of our outside footwear. Have indoor shoes prepared on the door, or inside the porch, and have strict effects (toilet scrubbing, and so on) for people who transgress.

Sock Puppet Dusters

Yes, take the tough workout session of dusting with the beneficial aid of giving it to the kids to do. OK, even in case you can't consider them near sensitive ornaments and have to do the process your self, socks make splendid dusters! Use an antique pair which have been washed, ones with holes in are quality. You can dust blinds via blending up an answer of water and vinegar (same factors) and dip on sock on this, run it along the blind, on foot the dry sock alongside afterwards to dry. This is a totally powerful approach and definitely brief! For fashionable dusting you can use favored spray or the water/vinegar method to rapid and with out hassle get all of the ones areas that everyday dusters find out it difficult to attain. The cloth is just as effective as ordinary dusters and it is a miles much much less costly choice in the long term.

Carpet Cleaning

While our kitchens and toilets may be the maximum intently used rooms in our homes, the carpets round our homes really do get the worst of all worlds! Constantly underfoot and continuously prone to spills and staining, they may quickly begin to appearance tired and worn. You can lease a carpet purifier or cleansing company to revitalize them however you can moreover remedy many problems yourself. For stubborn stains, baking soda may be your biggest fine buddy. Especially nearly approximately oily stains from food, really sprinkle some soda over the offending vicinity and leave for ten to 15 minutes. Vacuum as normal and repeat if essential.

All Purpose Cleaner

For an powerful, homemade cleanser, use this recipe:

- 2 cups of borax

- 1 cup of baking soda

- ½ cup of citric acid

- ½ cup of coarse salt

- some drops of your favored essential oil

Mix all the substances collectively and then keep in a Mason Jar or a sprig bottle. To use the spray sincerely have a look at to the floor to be wiped smooth, go away it for a couple of minutes and easy off with a humid material. The mixture is non-toxic and secure to apply in most elements of your house. Borax is a in fact occurring mineral chemical compound and at the same time as it's miles steady (it may be positioned in cosmetics or even meals in some countries) it's far nice no longer saved wherein it is available to kids or animals.

Fan Dusting with the Hassle

Dusting a ceiling fan is in reality no a laugh. As hard to reach areas go it's miles had been given to be excessive at the listing. Use a pillowcase to dust the blades! Simply location over the entire blade and pull the case away. Done cautiously this can take away the dust, with out leaving it everywhere within the ground and/otherwise you!

Mattress Cleaners

Sadly, you can not certainly pop your mattress in the washing system. However, to cast off smells and dirt mites (a large purpose of allergic reactions) you can create your private bed cleanser. Use a cup of baking soda combined with ten drops of vital oil. In this case, use Lavender or Eucalyptus oil, every are natural trojan horse repellents that mites hate. Dust lightly over the bed and go away to take a seat down for multiple hours in advance than vacuuming off to dispose of the powder. This freshens, deodorizes and repels dust mites; repeat as required but it's miles genuinely worth doing on every occasion you exchange and wash the sheets.

Wood Polish

Forget the pricey timber polishes for optimum family woodwork. A simple domestic made spray will do. Mix the subsequent materials and upload to a sprig bottle to be used as required;

- 2 tablespoons of olive oil

- ¼ cup of white vinegar

- 2 cups of water

- essential oil to scent (non-obligatory)

The cleansing spray is outstanding for timber and includes the equal simple factors as many commercially to be had spray polishes. It's furthermore proper for maximum circle of relatives surfaces.

Spiders and Ants

These unwelcome site visitors are often located in many houses. You should buy specifically poisonous substances to rid your own home of them but maximum people do now not virtually just like the usage of this approach. If you have got kids and/or pets, you can probable pick out to limit the huge kind of deadly chemical compounds you operate round the house. For spiders, mix up your own, non-poisonous, spray to look them off. One cup of vinegar, combined with a teaspoon of oil, one in every of liquid soap and a cup of cayenne pepper will make a secure, natural spray. Simply spray as required spherical home windows and doorways. Repeat as critical.

Ants may be continual, however, our antique pal baking soda can come to the rescue. Mix the soda with sugar; the ants cannot face up to the sugar, munching the combination up greedily and then returning with some to the nest. At first look this could sound like you're genuinely feeding the ants and provoking them. Sadly, for the ants as a minimum, the baking soda reacts with herbal acids inside the ant's body and the reaction kills them.

Quick Car Cleaning Hacks

Homemade Air Freshener; use a bit of felt lessen right right into a spherical (or pine tree shape, if you like authenticity) pierce with a whole and infuse with important oil of your choice.

Baking soda isn't simply constrained to the residence; vacuum the car seats, then sprinkle baking soda over them. Leave it to sit down down for an hour and then vacuum once more. The deodorizing qualities of baking soda are endlessly beneficial!

Especially in wintry weather situations, the usage of can be daunting. Dirt, dirt and grit can fast constructing up on the headlamps and having the ones smooth and clean may be essential for night time riding.

Chapter 17: Speed Cleaning one zero one

Cleaning the residence is quite a time-consuming affair, making it hard for you if you have a hectic time table. However, this commonly does no longer must be the case. You can despite the fact that hold your private home clean no matter absolutely half-hour of cleansing. (But endure in mind that you but want to deep clean now and again to ensure that dirt underneath chairs and distinctive device does no longer gather.) Before we get started on pace cleaning, it is critical which you are privy to critical cleaning resources as that is essential to retaining a house clean.

The Basic Cleaning Supply List

Dusting Supplies

Dusting is essential, but its frequency will rely on your décor, way of life and incidence of any hypersensitive reaction and breathing troubles on your family. The tools can even range along side your non-public alternatives, but the following kinds can are to be had in on hand:

i) Microfiber clothes, for complex and trendy dusting

ii) Dusting spray

iii) Vacuum cleanser dusting attachment for corners, partitions and excessive ceilings

iv) Furniture polish

Trash Supplies

Even with the smallest of own family, there may be typically the opportunity of quite a bit of waste and trash in the house. While the ones equipment are smooth, they will be vital for going for walks your own family easily. Here are the equipment:

i) Trash can liners (each save sold liners or reused grocery sacks)

ii) Trash cans

iii) Recycling bins

iv) Baking soda

General Surface Cleaning Supplies

Every ground in your room receives dirty, and that may be a reality. Therefore, you want an tremendous cleaner to keep all the sticky spots, spills and smudges easy. The great tool for this task is a incredible all-reason purifier. However, an extra one or cleaners can are to be had in handy for well-known cleansing. Here are a few tips:

i) Kitchen cleaner or wipes

ii) All-cause cleanser

iii) Sponges, cleaning garments, paper towels

iv) Bathroom purifier or wipes

v) Gloves

vi) Scrubbers

Special Surface Cleaning substances

If your home is like many others, you probably have numerous surfaces that want specific hobby even as cleansing them. While those surfaces have a tendency to offer your property spice and range, having a awesome idea of what to do with them can be a touch demanding.

The following products can help:

i) Stone cleaner

ii) Oven cleaner

iii) Dish detergent

iv) Dish soap

v) Wood polish

vi) Leather cleanser

vii) Upholstery spot remover

viii) Laundry cleaning soap

ix) Laundry components

x) Laundry stain remover

xi) Toilet bowl purifier

xii) Air freshener

xiii) Soft scrubbing remover

xiv) Glass cleanser

xv) Metal or silver polish

xvi) Bleach

(Back to top)

The Living Room

Nothing cramps up a excellent night time time like a living room entire of cluttered mess after the visitors have departed, or while the children have lengthy long beyond to bed. Just at the same time as you are about to unwind for a chunk on the identical time as, you test the dwelling room and also you see a bookshelf, sofa, the ground and the espresso desk in desperate need of help. Fortunately, you can rework this hopeless mess in the residing area in only a few mins and still have a few minutes left.

1.Gather your belongings. Like with all rooms, this is one of the maximum vital steps. Having all your additives accessible earlier than cleaning manner minimal distractions within the course of the cleaning technique.

2.After gathering your essential substances, the following step is to place all the gadgets in a bin and place them outside the dwelling room for some time. Do not return the gadgets to their respective storage regions but, as you may waste time scurrying throughout the residence a couple of instances placing every object in its rightful place. Do this after you have got dusted the area.

3.Organize the couch then dismiss the cushions after which extract any gadgets from underneath the couch. Remove the dust from the indoors of the sofa and replace or fluff the pillows.

four.Dust the coffee desk and arrange the contents nicely. Keep in mind that the problem here is to dismiss the desk rapid and stack its contents smartly. Do now not worry about making the furniture shine meticulously, or arranging the coffee desk books alphabetically. Simply set up the books and magazines nicely.

five.Sweep or vacuum the floor. Do no longer float any furniture at the same time as doing this, or even as vacuuming the couch and pillows. You can do the ones in depth if you have more time. However, bear in mind to take care of the dirt you brushed from the interior of the couch in advance on.

6.Keep apart your broom, vacuum or dust rag. Breathe and take a second to experience your new residing room. Does it appearance any superb from in which it turned into fifteen minutes inside the past?

Chapter 18: How to Prevent Dust from Accumulating

The living room can be pretty dusty; as a quit result, you can want to comprehend the way to lessen the dirt in the domestic.

Use Entrance Mats

Place double the front mats in any respect the front and exit factors to prevent dirt — one outdoor the door and the other proper internal. Be high-quality to pick out out mats which might be durable sufficient to stand as much as everyday net web page visitors in your private home and don't forget to smooth the mats frequently. Also make sure they are slip-proof — tack them or select out one with rubber lining.

Change Air Filters

Make a dependancy of tracking the scenario of your air filters to envision if they are nevertheless going for walks well.

Most air filters have a lifespan of between one and 3 months, however you want to exchange them as speedy as they may be clogged with debris and dust. Changing air filters will now not fine lessen dirt in your property, however it'll make bigger the lifespan of your aircon machine, giving it an easy time cooling your property. You can also additionally even reduce your power invoice and gain regular extraordinary air in your private home.

Brush Pets

Make a difficulty of brushing your pets on a normal foundation to reduce dropping. For maximum pup owners, a variety of the debris and dirt originates from the pets. Apart from lowering the amount of losing and dander in your private home, this step may additionally even provide you with brilliant time together with your pet. Incorporate a ordinary bathing habitual on your puppy to reduce puppy dander.

Remember to smooth up the domestic dog bedding regularly in addition to the pet areas.

Keep the Windows Shut

When domestic windows are shut, it's going to prevent debris and dust from blowing into the house. In addition, it's miles typically an outstanding idea to test to your door and window climate stripping at least as soon as a year to examine if it is though functioning well. Replace any vintage weather stripping to enhance the seals for your doors and windows.

Select Good Quality Tools

While severa dusting merchandise exist within the marketplace, each one has its very personal professionals and cons. Find the right dusting device for cleaning up. Microfiber cloths are specially to be had as they lure even the tiniest of dust debris. Electrostatic dusters and lambs wool are also famous for a similar motive. However, most human beings pick a vacuum cleaner for dusting because it sucks all the dirt debris.

Use Slipcovers

These are notable in your upholstery as you can shake out a slipcover in contrast to whilst vacuuming dirt from a whole couch. The pleasant element is that you will moreover be shielding your furniture from accidental spills. Look out for a slipcover that is simple to care and one which you may with out problem address.

Do Not Over-Polish

If you use a furnishings polish or oil, ensure you examine the manufacturer's suggestions. Overusing the product can cloud your timber surfaces or motive a building up on your furniture. A dry microfiber can come in accessible because it options up extra dirt and forestalls the fixtures from being clouded or having a buildup of oily materials.

Repair Wood Surfaces

Take benefit of dusting time to restore any seen scratches to your timber furniture. A fixtures crayon or marker can are available available at the same time as going over the scratches in some unspecified time within the destiny of the dusting approach. Use this time to cast off adhesive stains, burn stains or candle wax out of your fixtures too.

Use Fabric Softener Sheets

You can recycle material softener sheets to dirt in area of the steeply-priced electrostatic cloths.

Start From Top to Bottom

 A accurate technique whilst dusting is to begin from pinnacle to bottom to keep away from repeating surfaces more than as soon as. Some times may additionally furthermore warrant wet dusting after dusting, but make sure you begin through dry dusting first. Watch out for timber surfaces whilst wet dusting as they may warp, stain, or perhaps become broken.

Useful Cleaning Tips

•If you have had been given a few minutes to spare after vacuuming, acquire the out of place items in a topic and take them to their garage rooms. This will simplest take a few minutes, however you may be glad while morning comes.

•If there is not a good deal litter on your dwelling room, use the spare time to rush vacuum the interior of your couch while you are finished with the ground.

(Back to pinnacle)

The Kitchen

One of the busiest rooms and the best that goals normal interest maximum might be your kitchen. However, if you are not careful, you may end up cleansing the kitchen numerous times in an afternoon. Fortunately, there is a way to show all this around in best fifteen mins, and bring your kitchen from the grimy cavern it is to a glowing smooth haven.

What You Need

•Basket for objects that don't belong inside the kitchen

•Other cleaners you usually use

•Scrubber for caught-on food

•Trash subject

•Dish cleaning cleaning soap

•Dishrag or sponge

•Broom, mop, or vacuum

Cleaning Up

1.Gather all the crucial additives. Most human beings underestimate the fee of this step. Trying to find sponges, dishcloths, cleansers, and masses of others while cleansing can devour up masses of some time and increase the opportunities of distractions, which can make you unfastened interest on what you had been doing within the first area.

2.Fill a sink with warmness and soapy water. If your sink doubles as a garbage disposal on one side, you may want to apply the disposal free detail so you can scrape the leftovers down the drain at the same time as you discern quick.

3.Scrape each dish into the rubbish disposal or trash. If your disposal has been blocked from the preceding step, use a dirty plate to scrape the dishes off.

4.Put the dishes that need to be soaked into the water. Select the dishes that appear to have the maximum cussed stains for both you or your dishwasher to deal with. The carefully dirty dishes need to live at the bottom. Fill the big dishes along facet bowls and pans with warm, soapy water, and area them at the counter to soak.

5.Leave the soaked dishes and undergo the kitchen as you smooth out any trash from your cabinets, counter tops, floor, and so forth. Do not trouble approximately the devices that look like out of vicinity or aren't speculated to be inside the kitchen; popularity exceptional on the trash.

6.Proceed to build up all the items that are not presupposed to be within the kitchen, and placed them in a basket. If you have got a helper like your companion or kids, allow them to positioned away those gadgets. Let no longer taking the out of vicinity objects to their garage rooms distract you from running at the kitchen.

7.Next, acquire all of the out of area gadgets that belong inside the kitchen and go back them to their rightful locations. Try now not to get distracted with the rearrangement of the drawers, cabinets, and lots of others. Just region the out of place gadgets to their storage area and hold.

eight.Clean the dishes.

9.You can each use the dishwasher or wash them with the useful resource of hand. If a dishwasher is to be had at domestic, then it may take you extra time to complete cleansing the dishes. Alternatively, you may gather an meeting line if possible with a couple of exclusive human beings to clean, rinse, dry and placed away the dishes. You may also additionally even use this time to chat and capture up at the side of your circle of relatives people.

10. Wash down your sink, domestic device and counter tops. Rinse out your rags and sponges, and if critical, aggregate them with the grimy garments. This is not heavy duty cleansing, however sincerely cleaning the seen surfaces. Rather than beginning the microwave and scrubbing it out or cleansing out the crumbs from the toaster, simply wipe it down quick with a smooth moist cloth.

11. Sweep down and mop, or vacuum.

12. Take out the trash. If day after today is trash day or the trash is full, take it out of doors and prepare the trash discipline for the following day's trash.

Some Helpful Tips

1.If there are many human beings in your property, it might take more time to complete the cleaning technique. However, this is additionally a hidden advantage, as this indicates greater participants to your cleaning marketing campaign. Create a regular out of the smooth up way, and divide the chores among the own family people. You will locate cleansing the kitchen faster and interesting.

2.Instill in your family participants the addiction of cleaning up and rinsing their very personal dishes after every meal. This will now not most effective take a short time for man or woman plates, however it will furthermore keep loads of time for the person who finishes very last.

3.Prepare a sink of heat and soapy water earlier than you begin making your food. This manner, you can brief wash the knives, reducing forums, mixing bowls, and so forth, as soon as possible to prevent them from sticking when they dry.

4.Make up a music collection for the own family clean up, and allow each family member make contributions a favorite tune. This is also a first-rate manner to get the youngsters concerned. Letting them pick out the songs ought to cause them to enjoy like they have got an input into the system.

NB: This is every day protection cleanup designed to keep time. You can also use it for a fast restore if you have some sudden visitors on the way.

(Back to top)

Chapter 19: The Bedroom

The bed room might be the maximum crucial room in your own home. As such, this area must be your sanctuary, the location wherein you land up at the surrender of the day. However, most of our rooms were transformed into garage areas, which make it unpleasant for all of us else to go into. The right facts is that you turn most of these round using a quick cleanup approach. Here is how:

1.Gather all your elements. These are what you could need:

•A vacuum purifier or broom

•A trash box

•A basket, bin, or discipline to place litter gadgets

•A obstruct

2.Collect all of the dirty clothes and located them in a impede. As you're in a hurry, do not problem about turning the shirts proper element out or unrolling the socks. You can try this at the same time as you're sorting the laundry. Just placed all of the grimy clothes and stash them in a avoid, then waft on.

three.Gather all of the easy apparel and re-cling or refold. If there are plenty of easy clothes prepared to be folded, you could bypass this step and pile them neatly for your mattress after you have got got made it for folding later.

four.Gather all the trash and positioned it in the rubbish can. Do no longer use this time to parent out whether or not or no longer to trash antique magazines or newspapers. The point right here is to pay attention only on the apparent trash, and no longer locating out closets and containers. You can kind out the alternative gadgets when you have sufficient time.

5.Make the mattress. If you discover it a waste of time making the bed, humor me. Since you can bounce once more into mattress in a few hours, there may be no want to make it, right? Wrong! If you used that argument for the opposite regions of your house, you'll in no way have smooth laundry, dishes, or floors. Why want to you smooth some thing at the same time as it is going to get dirty all yet again? The exceptional cause to make the bed is that it adjustments the appearance of a room, to appearance uncluttered and inviting.

6.Pick up all of the gadgets that do not belong within the mattress room. Grab all the out of area gadgets at the desk, floor, bed, and so forth and located them in a bin, subject, or basket. Do no longer move approximately putting them again one after the other; honestly accumulate them in a single vicinity and drift on, for now.

7.Straighten surfaces. If it's far been some time for the cause that final time you wiped smooth up, there can be certain to be masses of stuff in the room that are not in their rightful storage areas. Take a test the ones gadgets. If it's miles viable to area all of it away in simplest a minute or a good deal less, achieve this. Otherwise, gather all the objects and put them in a subject to type it out later.

eight.Sweep and vacuum or mop, but do now not bypass the fixtures even as sweeping or vacuuming. A brief run through will do for now.

9.Set aside your materials. When all of the approach is completed, stand lower again and reflect on how heaps one in each of a kind the charge-wiped easy room is. Repeat this process regular and you will slowly make the room spotless.

Useful Cleaning Tips

1.If you have a couple of minutes to spare, take the gadgets in the hampers and positioned them once more to their rightful garage areas.

2.Keep the miscellaneous baskets in mind so you don't leave them unattended for too extended. Doing this can in the end cause an overspill, this means that that more cluttered mess. If sorting them out now might be out of the query, use tomorrow's fifteen mins to achieve this.

3.Do not neglect approximately the easy clothes you place apart to fold later. Placing them on the mattress is a great way to take into account to fold or grasp them in some time.

(Back to pinnacle)

The Kids' Bedroom

If you have got were given youngsters in your own home, you can have located that their idea of pace cleaning is pretty one in every of a type from what it honestly is. For them, tempo cleansing manner smoothing out the dirt ruffle and shoving each cluttered object underneath the bed. Provide a actual cleanup method on your youngsters that allows you to take pleasant fifteen minutes, but go away their room simply purifier. The following steps can help get your teen's room in extraordinary form, and no one will need to give up a full Sunday.

1.Gather your elements. Find a garbage can, abate or toy field, in case you do not already have them for your room. Here are the crucial necessities:

- A bin, subject or basket to place the clutter devices

- Hamper

- Vacuum cleaner or broom

- Toy container

- Trash box

Avoid starting the cleansing way earlier than you've got all the sources to hand. Trying to find one supply at a time can waste severa some time.

2.Gather all of the grimy garments and located them in a impede. Having your grimy garb close to the preclude isn't always pinnacle sufficient; they want to be inside the impede. Do no longer attention on turning the clothes proper thing out or unfolding your socks. That will come later when you are finding out the laundry.

3.Gather all the trash and placed it in the garbage can. Try to awareness nice at the trash at this 2nd, and choose up all the apparent trash.

four.Make the bed. Most human beings discover making the mattress a whole waste of time. Just smooth out the sheets, then the blanket or comforter and fluff your pillows. Now, if you stand once more and look again on the mattress, it appears an entire lot neater, right? And except, you're lots less probable to lose stuff for your bed when you have smoothed it out.

5.Gather all the clean garments and re-cling or refold them. You will want your previously made mattress for this step. If there are numerous garments to be folded or hanged, genuinely pile them for your bed to fold them later so that you recollect. This will no longer best save you some time inside the inside the meantime, however it'll moreover hold the room searching neat. In addition, the stack of garments at the mattress will remind you to fold them proper in advance than crawling to bed.

6.Collect all the toys from the ground, under the bed, desk, and so on, and placed them everywhere they belong, whether it's miles a domestic dog net, or toy field. Do no longer consciousness on grouping the toy pieces together; really promote off they all into the field. Organizing can come later.

7.Gather all of the devices that do not belong within the teen's room and positioned them in a bag, vicinity or basket. Do not worry approximately placing the devices again to their storage spaces. For now, simply stuff them in a basket.

8.Vacuum or sweep and mop, but do not consciousness on shifting the mattress and shelves for this step.

nine.Put aside all your components, and you're completed! Look lower lower back at the room from the door. Does it appear like a place you will truly want to live in?

Some Helpful Tips

1.If you have got a few minutes to spare after cleaning, older youngsters can take the gadgets in the basket to their rightful regions. Younger kids can certainly location the basket within the hall on the manner to come and type it later.

2.Be cautious while leaving the devices within the basket. With regular little cleanups, in the long run you will discover the basket overflowing with devices. Thus, you will want to de-clutter and prepare weekly.

three.Train your younger children to encompass the brand new cleanup method through having them help out every day for in line with week.

four.Prepare a photo chart if you have a younger child to help them follow the important steps to a a achievement tempo cleansing method.

5.You may additionally moreover need to apply a visible praise chart to signify whether or not or not the children have performed their cleanup every day, and reward them at the surrender of the month.

(Back to pinnacle)

The Bathroom

As a full-size rule of thumb, your rest room desires to be wiped smooth frequently. Unfortunately, the cleanup machine isn't always as easy as choosing up items to make it neat, in assessment to different rooms. However, you could though maintain your rest room easy the use of the subsequent pace cleansing steps without slaving away for hours disinfecting and scrubbing each part of the relaxation room. Your children too can use this technique while not having to labor all day extended.

1.Gather all the wished materials. As stated formerly, having all of the important property on hand can prevent masses of time arising from all of the distractions. Taking a time out to seize the broom can sway you into checking the mail, which ultimately inclines you to record some of it and you all at once come across a letter that reminds you to call a relative. Sooner or later you recognize that the rest room is the final problem for your mind, and it's far too late. The excellent technique is to concentrate on one venture at a time.

Here is what you'll want:

•Broom and mop

•A trash area

•Glass Cleaner and rag

•Toilet Cleaner

•A basket, bin, or field to put litter gadgets

- A bog down

- Disinfectant wipes

- Toilet brush

2.Gather all of the grimy clothes and placed them in a bog down. Try not to get distracted through something however the grimy garments, even though it is throwing away the trash. Just focus on the dirty garments, however do now not problem unfolding pant legs or turning the socks proper side out. Throw all grimy garments in the impede.

3.Grab all the trash and toss it into the trash can, but as traditional, try to interest most effective on the obvious trash.

4.Wipe down the bath place and sink using a disinfectant. The component proper here is to supply lower returned the sink and tub into an ordered bliss to appearance presentable. Wipe down the bath casually; but positioned more time on the sink. You can also want to put on disposable gloves to defend your self whilst cleansing the relaxation room efficiently with out stressful too much approximately what you touch.

5.Scrub the inner of the bathroom in quick at the aspect of your chosen toilet cleanser and a relaxation room brush. Remember, this isn't always a complete scrubbing of the bathroom. It is in reality maintaining the relaxation room from where you left it final. This is also a extraordinary approach if you have sudden business organization on the manner to make the toilet look presentable.

6.Wipe the outside of the relaxation room with the assist of a disinfectant wipe. It takes a couple of minutes to run over the out of doors of the toilet the usage of the wipe. Just supply attention to removing the plain dust.

7.Wipe down the reflect with vinegar or a tumbler cleaner. A amazing way to hold the replicate easy regular is to put a touch time into this step every on occasion, even if in a rush. Guests have a propensity to spend pretty a while at the reflect, so they may in the end observe streaks and dinginess.

8.Collect all the items that don't belong in the relaxation room and placed them in a bin, difficulty, or basket.

nine.Gather all of the items that belong within the lavatory and positioned them lower returned into their storage regions. Do not fear approximately reorganizing the linen or treatment shelves; without a doubt placed once more the objects wherein they belong. You can come decrease lower back and arrange if you have greater time.

10. Mop or sweep. Just give attention to the precept foot website traffic vicinity and sweep the ground in brief. You might also even use a Readymop, Swiffer or a similar device to mop the ground in just a few seconds.

11. Keep aside your materials. Now, take 3 seconds while your bathroom is executed and surprise at your organization. It seems a lot better, proper?

Clean Up Tips

• If you use the ones steps to hold your rest room regular, every fifteen minutes you use to easy up will drift loads faster with each day.

• Make a component of collecting your bathroom resources earlier than you start cleansing. Hunting for elements everywhere inside the house can devour up loads of some time and amplify the pastime. In addition, observe greater caution whilst storing unstable chemicals in which both your pet or children can reap them.

(Back to pinnacle)

Chapter 20: The Garage

The garage is one of the hardest places to clean up, and in most times, it requires a dedicated day for effective de-cluttering. The most important issue is to have a plan, however inside minutes, you may efficiently supply again your garage to reserve. Here is how:

Speed-Cleaning the Garage

Look on the Deep Space

Generally, a darker storage tends to accumulate more clutter. This is broadly speaking because of the idea, "out of sight out of mind". The incredible method is to pick out out a sunny day to mild up the space and then step lower returned and observe. For now, honestly attention on the gadgets caught within the middle of the garage, proper approximately the vicinity in which the auto is supposed to move, and store the relaxation for when you have more time.

Hang It Up

Begin by the usage of shifting everything inside the center location, collectively with the hoses, garden chairs, extension cords, and so forth, up onto wall hooks. On the opposite hand, if putting is not an alternative, you can in reality line up the objects in competition to the partitions.

Get in In the Bin

You do not need fancy bins — absolutely what you've got, whether or now not it's miles planters or flowerpots. These are in particular superb for stray gardening gloves and collecting pruners. Additionally, you may furthermore use one or two garbage cans for hockey sticks, baseball bats and lengthy-handled brooms, similarly to a laundry basket for helmets and gear like balls.

Bag It

The subsequent step is to open up trash sacks; one for tossing any rusty, empty or broken objects, and the opportunity for containing things that do not belong inside the garage. You do not must positioned the whole lot another time in place currently, simply interest on amassing the objects for now.

Be Smart about Stains

Now that the floor is without trouble seen, oils splotches must now be first rate. Sprinkle oil stains with kitty litter if the stains are although sparkling – permit it absorb, after which sweep away the stains. You might also moreover need to easy thoroughly if they'll be already dry, which isn't simply at the time desk these days.

Clean Sweep

The very last step is to capture a dustpan brush or broom and begin putting off any bugs and cobwebs which have accrued on the door, walls, ceiling, and for the duration of the mild fixtures. Sweep the whole lot to the middle and then push particles and leaves out of the garage right away, and you are performed!

(Back to top)

How to Get Motivated to Clean Up

One of the most obvious limitations to cleaning up is the dearth of motivation to jumpstart the cleansing technique. As such, this leads to build up of litter from eventually's mess to the following. Before you apprehend it, you're residing in a house complete of scattered clothes, toys everywhere and numerous old magazines piled up at the coffee desk. In order to keep your property smooth and prepared, it's miles quality to live inspired; in any other case, you may constantly do away with these days's mess until it finally gets out of hand.

Motivate Yourself

Here are some useful tips to get stimulated:

Listen to Music

Music is a superb motivator to get you started out on the cleaning technique, whether or not you choose an mp3 participant, the radio or your very private playlist from the computer. Upbeat track is the fine for cleaning, because it will make you determine faster. The brought gain is which you also get some mild exercise inside the manner.

Wear Comfy Clothes

It does not usually need to be your terrific garments, but neither does it have to be pajamas. Wearing snug shoes can really hold your mind in a running mode. Cleaning for your strolling shoes and denim pants need to make it difficult so that it will take the art work severely. Comfy clothes gets the artwork completed faster.

Set a Deadline

One right way to set a limit for your self is to invite humans over for dinner on a positive date. This way, cleaning and organizing will continuously be behind your mind. You gets stimulated to get the house so as. However, make certain you deliver your self a sensible closing date to get the cleansing in truth performed. If critical, use a timer. Kids are mainly keen on this, and they'll normally get captivated with searching for to beat the clock.

Read Housekeeping Articles

These are tremendous resources to get the pointers and motivation had to get you started out out. This will are available in accessible specially at the same time as organizing the house. Just don't get too engrossed within the ebook/article that you clearly neglect to easy.

Tour a Model Home

Surveying photographs of houses in magazines or journeying a model domestic may be a splendid deliver of motivation to smooth too. While the ones are definitely standards for the reason that no one surely is living in them, they'll let you envision a outstanding home, imparting you with the inducement to reach for that ultra-modern.

Try a New Product

Having a state-of-the-art heady scent or cleaning product can actually get you more inspired to start cleansing. This is specially right if the product is designed to save you time or cash. Everyone is constantly looking for deals, specifically in these areas. Therefore, the subsequent time you are lazing on the concept of scrubbing your showerhead, appearance out for a ultra-modern product to your cleaning aisle. It may probable prove to be fun at the same time as attempting it.

Exchange Cleaning Time with Pals

The most effective way this can artwork is with a notable buddy that you recall. However, buying and selling cleansing obligations can be very motivating, extra than even cleansing your personal house. You may also try a joint organizing/cleansing consultation together together together with your pal, in which one Saturday is at your location, and the alternative at your pal's house. You would in all likelihood even persuade every specific to do away with some of the objects cluttering your closets and shelves.

Involve the Whole Family

Schedule some time on one Saturday for cleansing or organizing and tell the complete circle of relatives. A proper way to make this art work is to set apart a praise whilst the technique is completed. This may be a searching for journey, a movie or dinner. Give every family member a chance to manipulate the track, and characteristic some limited task options to maintain all and sundry glad inside the paintings pressure.

Organize a Garage Sale

This is a outstanding manner to easy out litter. The top notch thing is which you get to get rid of the belongings you do now not need with a chance of getting some cash to buy a few detail else. Consider donating the final items to charity, and keep away from bringing a few issue again into the residence. You will discover even your children extra than happy to let bypass of a number of their stuff if there may be coins involved.

Reward Yourself

This can be a buy, which includes a e-book, or it can be committed time to perform a little issue you genuinely experience, which incorporates scrapbooking. Setting apart a praise while doing a dreaded task can be very motivating.

Chapter 21: Does This Sound Familiar?

Do you feel like you are constantly cleaning the house? Your existence is spent choosing up, clearing up, cleaning up, tidying up, after which an afternoon or two later, its lower once more to the manner it end up. So what are you able to do to make house cleaning easier? How can you are making this time ingesting undertaking masses much less stupid and greater inexperienced? Like maximum dad and mom, I bet you want there was a magic wand that you can just wave and, poof! - the house might be spic and span. You probably fanaticize about Mary Poppins wherein she snaps her arms to tidy up the nursery. Well, possibly the following outstanding hassle, is to discover a listing of cleansing hacks that you may use to make your property cleansing chores go by means of in a flash.

Let's start out with the two best hack for cleansing productivity:

1) Multitasking

This would possibly probably seem apparent, but maximum of the time at the same time as you easy the residence, you cognizance on one chore or mission at a time. This will make the complete technique drag on and on. Rather, begin 2 or three plenty of chores proper now and change them cleverly so that you can reduce your cleaning time in half of. As a start, you can pop a load of washing on and fill the sink with heat water to soak a few dishes. While that's going, you could stroll round with a duster and wipe off surfaces at the equal time as you de-clutter. Make your manner throughout the residence systematically clockwise or anticlockwise, and paintings your manner round decrease lower back to the kitchen.

2) Prevention

Yes, we've got were given all heard it earlier than – in case you remedy and tidy as you pass, your own home acquired't get that messy first of all. We all recognize how tough this is to certainly observe, specially while procrastination devices in, so what are you able to do to attempt to prevent the house getting out of hand in the first location? One concept is to provide your self a 5 minute day experience. Set apart a selected time of day and set a stopwatch or your cellphone alarm to transport off in 5 minutes. Then fake you are taking element in a trolley dash competition, and race spherical your own home choosing up toys, throwing papers away, and placing grimy dishes in the sink. You may be surprised at how a good deal you could get accomplished in a measly five mins and an advantage is which you get a piece of cardio achieved.

These 2 are the principle productiveness boosters that you can start off with that will help you smooth your house greater efficaciously and keep it from getting too out of hand inside the first location.

Chapter 22: Hacks for the Kitchen

Cleaning the kitchen is a grievous task, but it might be the maximum vital, as it's far in which you are making and deal with meals. It's a not unusual misconception that your kitchen is the cleanest location, however in fact, in case you don't be aware about proper cleaning conduct, germs and micro organism can run rebel. For example, the kitchen sponge has been positioned to have the most bacteria out of every other household item. This technique that you want to disinfect it after each use and replace it often. Antibacterial or disinfectant wipes are also to be had for wiping down surfaces and counters every day. To make kitchen cleansing now not look like the sort of large venture, right right here are the top 5 hacks to make your gadget much less complicated:

1)   Lemon Wedge your Sink and Taps

This is a clean manner to get your sink to look vivid and current another time, on the way to provide you with that top notch feeling while you enter your kitchen each day. Something about a smooth, brilliant kitchen sink, simply makes us sense better. Cut a lemon in half of and rub the juice everywhere inside the metallic. It cuts grease, disinfects and smells high-quality!

2)   Baking Soda and Vinegar

These trendy circle of relatives gadgets you've got in your cabinet will help you with a myriad of cleaning troubles. Mix a paste of a 1/2 of of a cup of baking soda with some teaspoons of water and use it on your sink, your oven door, your variety, or to your fridge. Let the paste dry virtually just so it definitely permeates the hard grease and dirt. Then spray with vinegar. Beware it's going to begin scorching! But that is precisely what you want, due to the fact because of this that you don't must scrub for hours. Once the vinegar has completed all of the tough be simply right for you, take a difficult sponge or steel wool and scrub the the rest of the dust. Wipe smooth with a microfiber fabric once clean.

3)   Hot vs Cold Water

Washing dishes wants to be the worst, maximum miserable, time consuming venture inside the kitchen, however you'll be making the challenge plenty greater hard via now not records the distinction among warm water and bloodless water for high-quality dishes. For caked on egg and milk that has been burnt proper right into a pan, warm water will make it worse. These objects are proteins and becomes extra resistant while in contact with warmth. Use cold water for cleaning egg, milk, yoghurt, caked on cheese or each distinct protein based totally definitely food item.

four)   Bowl of Vinegar within the Microwave

For the ones traumatic, difficult splatters of food, the super way to clean it's far to area a cup of water with 2 tablespoons of vinegar within the microwave for 5 minutes. It will loosen the dust and you could very with out troubles wipe it off.

5)   Cream of Tartar

This works wonders on stainless steel home machine. Make it proper right into a paste and rub it for your toaster, kettle, or fridge door with a tender material to do away with those grease splatters and grimy finger marks. Wipe it off yet again and you may have vibrant, smooth appliances.

We procrastinate whilst topics aren't smooth, or at the same time as it seems like the type of project to do. So, all you want to do is find out a manner to make cleaning the kitchen smooth.